NO. 4, SUMMER 1997

NEW DIRECTIONS FOR SCHOOL LEADERSHIP

Students Taking the Lead

The Challenges and Rewards of Empowering Youth in Schools

RICHARD H. ACKERMAN
University of Massachusetts Lowell
Harvard Graduate School of Education

EDITOR-IN-CHIEF

JUDITH A. BOCCIA
University of Massachusetts

EDITOR

STUDENTS TAKING THE LEAD: THE CHALLENGES AND REWARDS OF
EMPOWERING YOUTH IN SCHOOLS
Judith A. Boccia (ed.)
New Directions for School Leadership, No. 4, Summer 1997
Richard H. Ackerman, Editor-in-Chief

Microfilm copies of issues and articles are available in 16 mm and 35 mm, as well as
microfiche in 105 mm, through University Microfilms Inc., 300 North Zeeb Road,
Ann Arbor, Michigan 48106-1346.

ISSN 1089-5612   ISBN 0-7879-9864-8

NEW DIRECTIONS FOR SCHOOL LEADERSHIP is part of The Jossey-Bass Education
Series and is published quarterly by Jossey-Bass Inc., Publishers, 350 Sansome Street,
San Francisco, California 94104-1342.

SUBSCRIPTIONS: Please see Ordering Information on p. iv.
EDITORIAL CORRESPONDENCE should be sent to Richard Ackerman, The Principals'
Center, Harvard Graduate School of Education, 336 Gutman Library, Cambridge,
MA, 02138.

Jossey-Bass Web address: http://www.josseybass.com

Printed in the United States of America on acid-free recycled paper containing 100
percent recovered waste paper, of which at least 20 percent is postconsumer waste.

The International Network of Principals' Centers

The International Network of Principals' Centers sponsors *New Directions for School Leadership* as part of its commitment to strengthening leadership at the individual school level through professional development for leaders. The Network has a membership of principals' centers, academics, and practitioners in the United States and overseas and is open to all groups and institutions committed to the growth of school leaders and the improvement of schools. The Network currently functions primarily as an information exchange and support system for member centers in their efforts to work directly with school leaders in their communities. Its office is in the Principals' Center at the Harvard Graduate School of Education.

The Network offers these services:

- The International Directory of Principals' Centers features member centers with contact persons, descriptions of center activities, program references, and evaluation instruments.
- The Annual Conversation takes place every spring, when members meet for seminars, workshops, speakers, and to initiate discussions that will continue throughout the year.
- *Newsnotes*, the Network's quarterly newsletter, informs members of programs, conferences, workshops, and special interest items.
- *Reflections*, an annual journal, includes articles by principals, staff developers, university educators, and principals' center staff members.

For further information, please contact:

International Network of Principals' Centers
Harvard Graduate School of Education
336 Gutman Library
Cambridge, MA 02138
(617) 495-9812

Ordering Information

NEW DIRECTIONS FOR SCHOOL LEADERSHIP
This series of paperback books provides principals, superintendents, teachers, and others who exercise leadership at the local level with insight and guidance on the important issues influencing schools and school leadership. Books in the series are published quarterly in Fall, Winter, Spring and Summer and are available for purchase both by subscription and individually.

SUBSCRIPTIONS cost $52.00 for individuals (a savings of 35 percent over single-copy prices) and $105 for libraries. Prices subject to change. There are no shipping and handling charges on subscriptions.

SINGLE COPIES cost $25.00 plus shipping. There will be handling charges on billed orders. Call the 800 number below for more information.

SINGLE COPIES AVAILABLE FOR SALE

SL1   Every Teacher as a Leader: Realizing the Potential of Teacher Leadership, *Gayle Moller, Marilyn Katzenmeyer*

SL2   Boundary Crossings: Educational Partnerships and School Leadership, *Paula A. Cordeiro*

SL3   Schools for Everyone: A New Perspective on Inclusion, *Elizabeth A. Hebert*

SL4   Students Taking the Lead: The Challenges and Rewards of Empowering Youth in Schools, *Judith A. Boccia*

QUANTITY DISCOUNTS ARE AVAILABLE. Please contact Jossey-Bass Periodicals for information at 1-415-433-1740.

TO ORDER, CALL 1-800-956-7739 or 1-415-433-1767
. . . and visit our website at http://www.josseybass.com

Contents

The meaning and potential of student leadership in schools has not been widely examined by practitioners or researchers. A literature search for exemplary student leadership programs and an analysis of significant features in such programs yielded little useful data. The relative scarcity of relevant literature reflects a general lack of effective student leadership models in schools, even though the theme is typically prominent in statements of mission and goals. The author suggests that broader integration of leadership training and opportunities into school programs will allow educators to tap into the rich networks of peer influence that exist among adolescents and to give reality to the goal of citizenship education.

1

Introduction: The challenge of student leadership

Judith A. Boccia

IN THEIR REPORT *Breaking Ranks: Changing an American Institution,* the National Association of Secondary School Principals (NASSP) declares that "one word, 'leadership,' sums up what high schools need most. . . . Leaders combine knowledge, skills, and attitudes that manifest themselves in many ways. Leaders challenge convention. Leaders stir others into action. Leaders take risks, sometimes to their personal disadvantage. Leaders, in other words, may find themselves *Breaking Ranks* with the status quo. Furthermore, leaders build the capacity to sustain improvement so that it extends beyond their personal involvement" (1996, p. 96). The report calls for an expanded notion of school leadership, one that includes students as well as the principal, teachers, parents, and other adults.

NEW DIRECTIONS FOR SCHOOL LEADERSHIP, NO. 4, SUMMER 1997 © JOSSEY-BASS PUBLISHERS

"The leadership of students . . . enriches a high school and provides valuable experience for the young people who assume leadership roles" (p. 107).

Most educators in the United States would probably agree with the NASSP about the desirability of student leadership in schools. As a student educational goal, leadership development encompasses lessons from civics, communications, critical thinking, history, and a host of other disciplines; as an institutional value, student leadership reflects the practice of democratic principles that underlie American public education; and as an administrative structure, student leadership provides a dynamic, renewable resource for feedback and ideas about teaching, learning, and living in a school. It is no surprise that with such positive attributes, student leadership has become commonplace in school philosophy statements, especially at the high school level.

Informal sampling of high school principals, teachers, or students reveals, however, that student leadership in schools is not quite what many mission statements promise. The most familiar version of student leadership in middle and high schools involves the activities of a select group of youth chosen by popular vote or adult nomination for positions of prominence. Implicit in the use of the words *student leader* to define these students are previous academic, political, and social success as well as promising futures. In this sense, *leadership* connotes past or future personal achievement rather than skills of promoting achievement in others, which is central to the concept of leadership. The traditional notion of student leadership also suggests a preoccupation with certain kinds of activities, like planning social events, challenging school rules, and representing the student perspective in adult conversations. This kind of leadership, while benign in its effect, is deceptive in that it substitutes a kind of tokenism for what the NASSP describes as the qualities needed in the leaders of today and tomorrow.

What accounts for the gap between the kind of vibrant, productive, influential student leadership suggested in school mission statements and envisioned by the NASSP, and the reality of practice in many schools? Over the past decade, the theme of student leadership has often been discussed in a series of continuing development workshops with public school principals conducted by the Center for Field Services at the University of Massachusetts Lowell. During these workshops, high school principals have expressed important views regarding student leadership as well as explanations for the difficulty of developing and integrating student leadership in schools. Their conversations are summarized in the recreated dialogue that follows:

"Most kids don't see themselves as leaders, and they don't care enough about school issues to take on leadership responsibilities," said one principal.

"Well, I disagree about the caring," responded another. "The thing is, kids just don't have time to learn how to be leaders, or to do leadership stuff. What with jobs, activities, family commitments—most of our students are pretty committed already."

"Besides," chimed in a new voice, "by the time they do learn how to make a contribution, they've graduated! Then we just have to start over with a new group."

"And don't forget," admonished one principal, "it's definitely not cool to be seen as working with or for the administration. Unless you need it for your college application, you can't let anyone think school leadership matters."

"But leadership can be a meaningful part of the curriculum. The kids do get to participate in the democratic process. I have them on my site council, they go to the school committee, they get things done I can't do. They just can't get involved in professional things like curriculum and policies or confidential topics like personnel and finance. They don't know enough, and besides, the teachers would feel threatened."

"You're talking about the student government types, the editors, and presidents of clubs. They're no problem. My headache is the kids whose leadership undercuts what we're trying to do here—the gang leaders, the truants, the party crowd," commented another school leader. "We actually spend a lot of time trying to decrease their influence on other kids, what with suspension hearings, parent meetings, and court appearances. These negative leaders take up half my time."

"Mine too," agreed another principal. "And then there are all those kids who don't come to our attention as stars or troublemakers. But you know they have tremendous influence on each other in particular situations, like the class comedian, or the kid who forms his own band, or the one who can get tickets to any concert. We have no real role in that kind of leadership, and I don't know how we could."

"It's a shame, really," reflected one of the group. "If only we could harness all the energy kids spend in trying to beat or avoid the system, if we could make the system work for them, it would sure help us with our jobs, and we might actually feel like we're doing the job we got in this business to do—education!"

The insights, beliefs, and attitudes of these principals are a fair representation of the ambivalence surrounding the notion and practice of student leadership in schools. Young people who hold positions of school leadership usually receive their authority from and serve at the pleasure of administrators. Consequently, student responsibility is limited to those roles that adults have delegated. Further, positional student leaders, like student government and class officers, are often elected based on popularity rather than on some discernible ability to lead. They may or may not truly represent the student voice, may or may not be able to advocate on behalf of their peers, may or may not have influence with other youth. Other young people demonstrate peer leadership in a variety of ways not recognized by or accessible to the school. While some nonpositional leadership is negative in its impact on school culture, there is also great untapped potential for positive student leadership in many young people who do not run for office, join clubs, or play on teams. The principals who have participated in the Center for Field Services workshops would like to identify, develop, and integrate into their educational programs the kind of powerful peer influence that operates on the margins of school life. But effective models and methods for doing so are rare.

The principals have hinted at some reasons why student leadership has not evolved into the robust program for youth participation in school life that many of them have imagined:

- Young people are busy and their years in middle and high school are limited, so time to develop and practice leadership skills is short.

- Students have no knowledge base about many school issues nor any training to take leadership roles even if the knowledge were provided.
- The peer culture is cynical about youth leadership initiatives, often labeling student leaders as "narcs," "brownies," or similar unfortunate epithets.
- Teachers tend to resist involving students in professional matters, especially in the areas of curriculum and policy.
- It can be hard to engage youth concern about matters that have a time frame beyond the typical three- or four-year period of high school matriculation.
- Students have their own lives outside school and prefer to keep these worlds separate.

Although these explanations for the dearth of student leadership ring true, it is not clear how general they are or whether they represent insurmountable barriers to improving the extent and quality of student leadership in schools. If the traditionally perceived barriers are not insurmountable, what can be done to create a more robust practicum for student leadership? A look at the research literature reveals what others engaged in the study or practice of school leadership have learned.

The literature in brief

Extensive computer searches of library resources, long conversations with principals and students, frequent scanning of the popular press, and discussions with the directors of private sector and nonprofit youth organizations yields a surprisingly meager base of programmatic guidelines for successful student leadership in schools. The literature consists largely of leadership training models, studies of student leader characteristics, and cases of school leadership programs. Training models include several formats operating either within, completely outside, or in conjunction with schools. For example, the Future Farmers of America and Future

Business Leaders of America programs are cocurricular and career oriented, and are frequently operated in connection with academic departments, such as industrial arts or business. Other leadership training programs are run entirely outside the schools, often by industry or higher education agencies, and focus on individual youth talent development. Outdoor education programs, travel and study opportunities, and internships are typical of these extrascholastic leadership development efforts. Finally, a number of training programs are specific to students with a particular role to play in schools, like student government members, community service volunteers, peer mediators, team captains, and tutors. To further confuse an already ambiguous notion, the term *student leadership* is increasingly used as a synonym for self-efficacy in social service programs for youth at risk for academic failure and/or abusive behaviors. In general, many of these programs reinforce the concept of leadership as oriented to individual achievement. Relatively few programs focus explicitly on the development of capabilities to energize the efforts and talents of others, which is the core of leadership.

In addition to reports on various student leadership training models, the research includes some analysis of the behaviors and beliefs of young leaders. However, since many of these studies use as subjects administrator-selected student leaders, the findings are not particularly helpful in a search for new sources and kinds of student leadership in schools. Another avenue of research on leadership concerns the characteristics and skills of student leaders. Such research is a promising path for those developing curriculum or identifying prospective leaders, but it is not especially useful in clarifying how student leadership can be reimagined and renewed in schools.

The research is replete with anecdotal reports about the benefits of student leadership efforts in particular schools. By and large, these reports describe how students have been selected and trained to take an active role in programs of administrative, social, or community activities. Increasingly, peer mediation and violence prevention programs appear in this research category and offer promising avenues for finding student leaders among groups traditionally at the edges of school culture. To date, most of the peer mediation literature focuses on description of the programs and their effects on discipline incidents and school climate rather than focusing on the recruitment, training, and growth of the young people working as peer mediators. Very likely more attention will be paid to matters of peer leadership as mediation programs become institutionalized in schools.

The purpose of this issue

The scarcity of literature regarding student leadership creates a compelling rationale for this issue of *New Directions for School Leadership*. Despite the dearth of research on student leadership, the editors' persistent exploration yielded a number of exciting projects, a few inspiring young people, several principals committed to engaging youth in serious student leadership roles, and some provocative ideas about the value and potential of student leadership in schools. The chapters included in this issue represent a range of perspectives and programs involving student leadership. The writers capture the voices of students and principals on what student leadership means and on what is entailed in developing viable school programs. While no clear guidelines emerge from these chapters, there are common themes the understanding of which may help educators foster and support student leadership in a broader and deeper form than has traditionally existed in schools.

It seems clear from several of the cases presented, for example, that empowerment is a keystone of meaningful student leadership. Young people are given ownership and responsibility for some part of their school lives, and that empowerment is supported by a network of relationships with adults and peers. Whether they face the challenge of improving school climate, reputation, or programs, students in the schools described in this issue responded seriously and successfully to the tasks they were empowered to do.

Recognizing and developing leadership potential in students is another recurrent motif. Peer influence, rather than popularity, seems to be a hallmark of the student leaders who appear in the following chapters. These student leaders are capable of setting and staying on a course of action, and they attract others to their efforts. In communication with peers, the student leaders exhibit empathy for others' dilemmas and commitment to helping resolve those dilemmas.

School conditions that contribute to student leadership development and implementation are noted in several of the chapters. Trust, time, and training are required for the growth and practice of youth leadership. Integration of leadership development and application into school curriculum is one means of ensuring appropriate conditions for student leadership to emerge.

These ideas are illustrated, tested, and weighed here in attempts to clarify the meaning and potential for student leadership in schools. Regardless of how it surfaces and what shape it takes, the student leadership discussed in this volume is different than the traditional role of class or club officer. This is leadership of peer influence, responsive to community need, nurtured or supported by adults, and productive of personal as well as interpersonal change.

For school leaders seeking to redefine and recreate student leadership in their schools, the chapters included in this issue will provide ideas and resources for empowering youth as leaders. The compelling need to do so is expressed by the NASSP in its recent report: "The challenges of the final years of this century call for brave and courageous leadership to make certain that the future is determined by people who understand the genius of American democracy and prepare themselves to defend it" (1996, p. 107).

Reference

National Association of Secondary School Principals. *Breaking Ranks: Changing an American Institution* (#2109601). Reston, Va.: National Association of Secondary School Principals, 1996.

JUDITH A. BOCCIA is director of the Center for Field Services and Studies and a faculty member in the College of Education, University of Massachusetts Lowell.

This chapter discusses how one Connecticut high school has empowered students to take a leadership role in discouraging prejudice and discrimination. Student leaders have developed and implemented five programs: a student-led elementary education program, a high school prejudice reduction conference, a community prejudice reduction conference, social service projects, and student awareness programs. The student organization has become a model for other Connecticut schools addressing similar issues and has earned state recognition. Results of a recent evaluation show that students participating in the program benefit in several areas, including new knowledge about diverse cultural and religious groups, empathy for those discriminated against, and confidence in addressing issues of prejudice and other items.

2

The Human Relations Club: Student leaders addressing issues of multicultural education and social action

Scott Willison

IN RECENT YEARS, the fostering and maintaining of environments accepting of diverse populations has been a goal of schools and educators throughout the United States. However, in the often intense effort to make our schools equitable to everyone and to foster student acceptance of others, the role of the student is often one of passivity. Helping students to become not only knowledgeable and

NEW DIRECTIONS FOR SCHOOL LEADERSHIP, NO. 4, SUMMER 1997 © JOSSEY-BASS PUBLISHERS

accepting of others but also leaders in addressing issues of tolerance is of utmost importance. This chapter discusses how a group of empowered Hamden, Connecticut, high school students have taken an active leadership role in increasing the school's and the community's awareness of multicultural issues and in combating prejudice and discrimination. Included is a program description and a discussion of the program's impact on the student participants.

Schools can play a significant role in leadership development among our youth, and studies have shown that youth leadership experiences in school-based clubs can play a significant role in preparing youth for leadership as adults (Cox, 1988). Woyach (1992) states that to foster such leadership, schools must present youth with opportunities to connect to issues that concern them; they must be empowered to lead and to see themselves in a position to lead.

Multicultural education has garnered an extraordinary amount of attention, with much of the discussion addressing philosophical questions about its place in the curriculum (Cohen, 1986). Some researchers, such as Banks (1984), Willis (1993), Theel (1990), and others, present general guidelines for implementing a multicultural curriculum, while Grant (1994) and others identify how teachers are prepared to address multicultural issues in the classroom. However, as the National Council for the Social Studies has pointed out, the debate surrounding multicultural education has "generated more heat than light" (1992, p. 274). A review of the educational literature shows that while there are many discussions related to multicultural education, descriptions of comprehensive secondary programs and their effectiveness are less prevalent, and there exists very little discussion of students taking leadership roles in addressing related issues. Most of the multicultural learning activities discussed consist of discrete lessons organized around particular holidays and the contributions of specific individuals (Webb, 1990). Although within the literature there are examples of multicultural initiatives, such as Project Reach (Respecting Ethnic and Cultural Heritage), used in twelve states, and the Portland Public School multicultural initiative (Webb, 1990), there is a need for more information that addresses multicultural curricula beyond individual lesson plans, as well as the effectiveness of those curricula.

Hamden High School, a school of 1,560 students (21 percent minority) in grades 9 through 12, has been addressing multicultural issues since 1969 when, as *Time* magazine reported, race riots occurred in the school cafeteria ("Students and Now the High School," 1996). Since then, the Hamden School District (in particular, the Hamden High faculty), students, and parents have addressed multicultural concerns in a variety of ways. There have been ongoing revisions of the curriculum, faculty development days, parent and administration alliances, and the formation of a student organization, the Human Relations Club, or the HRC.

General overview of the HRC

In 1986, a school district initiative on equity included a series of speakers and workshops for faculty and students. It wasn't until 1990 that students, recognizing a need for increased and continuous student leadership in addressing issues of school cohesiveness, formed the HRC. The HRC continues to be a student-run organization that focuses on developing and implementing, within the school and community, ongoing activities designed to increase cultural, religious, and ethnic awareness and appreciation. The club also has a goal of reducing prejudice and discrimination within the school and community. The HRC has won recognition as the most extraordinary teen organization in the state of Connecticut, winning the Noxema Extraordinary Teen Award in 1994, and it can serve as a model for student involvement and ownership in addressing issues of multicultural education.

Since its inception, the HRC has grown to include a diverse population of 140 Hamden students, and it now works with student leaders from other school districts in forming new clubs. When Hamden students were questioned in a 1994 survey as to why they joined the club, three reasons were identified: they were concerned about issues that the club addresses, they had a desire to get involved in a school activity, and a friend was a member of the club. While the group's agenda is not always the reason given by students for joining the club, that the HRC is a multifaceted program offering many opportunities for participation and that members have the opportunity to shape its growth are significant factors in understanding the group's continuous high enrollment of students.

The central principle that has guided the HRC is the concept of students being empowered to make a difference. HRC advisors recognize that by permitting students to explore and pursue their ideas, they nurture a sense of responsibility and ownership within the students. The work that is done takes on a student-centered perspective rather than being teacher or advisor centered, and it develops social action agendas within the students. The benefits of social action have been documented by Conrad and Hedlin (1991), Lewis (1991), Willison (1994), and others.

Celebration of diversity: HRC programs

As an expression of their commitment to student empowerment and social action, HRC students since 1990 have identified five ways in which they can celebrate diversity and address prejudice, stereotyping, and other issues they have found prevalent in their daily lives. These programs are (1) the Prejudice Reduction Conference for middle and high school students, (2) the Community Prejudice Reduction Conference, (3) the Elementary Education Prejudice Reduction Program, (4) the Hamden High Social Service Program, and (5) a cultural awareness committee.

The Prejudice Reduction Conference for middle and high school students

The HRC sponsors an all-day spring conference for approximately three hundred high school and fifty middle school students. This annual event takes place at a local university. The conference has a professional format; students must register for the conference two months in advance and identify the particular workshops they are interested in attending. On the day of the conference, students are bused to the university, provided with a continental breakfast, given materials for the day, and addressed by a keynote speaker. They then participate in a ninety-minute session, have a free lunch, and attend a second ninety-minute session.

Over the years, conference sessions have had such titles as Combating Racism, Diversity in Relationships, Sexual Harassment, Living in the Hood, Understanding the Holocaust, Homophobia, Native American Issues, Religions of the World, and other topics that HRC members have identified as interesting to the student body. Once session topics are identified, the HRC conference committee members begin a process of identifying potential speakers who have expertise in the particular topics selected. HRC members contact all of the potential presenters, negotiate payment for their services, and communicate all logistical information through mailings to conference participants. HRC members are also responsible for selecting the lunch menu, developing and processing all registration information, and solving any last-minute problems that may arise. Although there is a faculty advisor to help, the majority of organization and implementation are done by the HRC members, who organize themselves into subcommittees. Conference planning begins in September and conference expenses are funded through the HRC's annual budget, which reflects Hamden Board of Education funding, grant monies, student fundraising, and corporate contributions.

To begin a dialogue with students from other school districts, HRC members invited ten other Connecticut schools to attend the 1994 conference. Approximately forty students and their faculty chaperons from seven of the invited schools attended the conference. As a result of their participation in the conference, five of the schools developed their own HRC organizations. To facilitate the development of the new programs, students from the two schools participate in Hamden's HRC events and consult with Hamden's student leaders.

Community Prejudice Reduction Conference

During the past five years, HRC members have become increasingly aware of the need to involve parents and the community in addressing multicultural issues. As a result of their concerns, a group of HRC members developed a Saturday conference for parents and other members of the community. The intent of the conference is to engage adults in conversation focused on multicultural issues and to provide them with some perspective on the lives of Hamden students. HRC members send notices home with all 5,500 students in the Hamden School District inviting parents to attend. They also advertise in local churches, in the newspaper, and by word of mouth. HRC members provide breakfast food and free child care while parents attend the conference. Participants go through a registration process, are addressed by a keynote speaker, and attend one of seven different sessions that explore issues such as Dealing with Prejudice Within the Home, Diversity Within the Family, The Work Force in the Year 2000, The History of African American Music, and others. In 1993, the first year of the Community Prejudice Reduction Conference, a survey of the one hundred adult participants revealed that 100 percent of them considered the conference valuable. As a result of the success of the conference, an organization made up of political, church, business, and other leaders from the local community has approached the HRC and offered to collaborate with them in the recruitment of participants for future community conferences. The conference is an example of how the high school students assumed a leadership role in developing a program and having an impact on the community.

Elementary Education Prejudice Reduction Program

For five years, members of the HRC have participated in a program designed to address multicultural issues at the elementary level. Each year, members of the HRC volunteer to attend weekly training sessions designed to increase their knowledge as it relates to multicultural issues and to learn specific teaching techniques that they will later use in an elementary classroom. During the 1995–96 academic year, seventy-four HRC members participated in this six-week program. A variety of techniques are covered, including the use of children's literature, role-playing, whole-class discussion, individual reflection, and hands-on activities. All of these techniques are used as catalysts for discussing issues such as racism, stereotyping, self-esteem, acceptance, and other related issues. The weekly training is developed and presented by the program's student leaders and by individuals with expertise in teaching about multicultural issues.

Once high school students have mastered the knowledge, strategies, and skills needed to teach elementary-age students about the concept of prejudice and related matters, they then attend a selected elementary school in the Hamden district once a week for six weeks. Each week, pairs or triads of trained students design and present a one-and-a-half-hour lesson for the class with which they are working. Elementary classroom teachers assist the HRC members only when necessary and often use the lesson as a tool for initiating discussion during the remaining portion of the week. As elementary students graduate into middle school and eventually into high school, their familiarity with the HRC acts as a catalyst to get them involved in their school and community, thus empowering a new generation of students to become school and community leaders in the fight against racism.

Hamden High School Social Service Program

Recognizing that there are many ways to address multicultural issues and that one of the best ways to develop an understanding of and care for the conditions of others is by working with individuals from diverse backgrounds, the HRC has initiated a social service program. Members of the HRC can participate in a variety of programs, including volunteering at one of New Haven, Connecticut's hospitals, participating in a buddy program pairing HRC members with special education students, serving in a tutoring/mentor program that pairs HRC members with urban youth six to twelve years old, working in an animal shelter, or working on a Habitat for Humanity project. HRC leaders are currently organizing other social service projects, such as making a monthly commitment to work at a food kitchen, being companions to senior citizens, and cooperating with a Meals on Wheels program.

Cultural awareness committee

Knowing that issues of racism, sexism, prejudice, and stereotyping need to be addressed within the school daily, some members of the HRC choose to participate on a cultural awareness committee. The purpose of the committee is to develop ways of addressing these issues regularly. HRC members plan events such as international dance presentations and field trips to see films such as *Schindler's List*.

Members of all the HRC projects gather at monthly meetings to discuss current issues as they pertain to the group, participate in prejudice reduction training, update each other on work being done in each committee, evaluate their efforts, and socialize. At those meetings students organize field trips to such places as the Holocaust Museum in Washington, D.C., and they develop fundraisers to pay for the trips.

Success of the Human Relations Club

In an attempt to evaluate the HRC's impact on its members, an anonymous survey was developed in the summer of 1994 and mailed to three hundred HRC members who had participated in the organization between 1991 and 1994. One third of the mailings were to former members who had graduated from Hamden High School, and the others were mailed to students who would be in grades 10 through 12 during the 1994–95 academic year. The survey asked participants to respond to seventeen questions, fourteen of which asked for a self-rating on a scale of "none," "little," "some," or "a lot" regarding the impact their participation in the HRC had on their recognition of racism, stereotyping, and inequity in their lives, and on how the HRC had helped prepare them to address instances of such behavior. Other questions asked students to identify their grade, their amount of participation in the HRC, why they joined the club, and the number of years they participated in it. The ninety-four responses (31 percent) were representative of the various groups to whom the survey was mailed. The statistical analysis of the returned surveys revealed no correlation between the responses and the age or grade of the respondent; however, when the responding criteria were given a numerical value, an analysis of the responses did reveal a correlation between those most involved in the club and those who reported the highest amount of gained insights and awareness of multicultural issues as well as comfortableness in addressing multicultural issues (see Tables 2.1 and 2.2).

Cultural insights

HRC members reported that participation in the club helped them gain new knowledge and information about other cultures and ethnic groups. While 51 percent of the respondents reported that because of their involvement in the HRC they had learned "some" about other cultures, 34 percent reported that they had gained "a lot" of new insight into other cultures (see Table 2.3). Within the HRC, cultural information is learned in a variety of ways, including through student panel discussions about the religious and cultural diversity found within the school, guest speakers discussing

Table 2.1. Correlation of students' perceptions of their involvement and insights gained with respect to cultural/religious groups and issues of racism, stereotyping, and prejudice

		*Average Response of Students Grouped by Level of Reported Involvement**	
Level of student involvement	*Number of student responses*	*New knowledge of cultural and religious groups*	*Help in clarifying issues of racism, etc.*
None	0	0	0
Little	13	2.69	3.0
Some	43	3.09	3.42
A lot	38	3.29	3.71

N = 94

Values of responses: none = 1, little = 2, some = 3, a lot = 4

Table 2.2 Correlation of students' perceptions of their involvement and reported willingness and confidence in accepting diverse perspectives in addressing issues of racism, stereotyping, and prejudice

		*Average Response of Students Grouped by Level of Reported Involvement**	
Level of student involvement	*Number of student responses*	*Willingness to consider different perspectives*	*Confidence in addressing issues of prejudice, etc.*
None	0	0	0
Little	13	3.15	2.77
Some	43	3.37	2.98
A lot	38	3.66	3.74

N = 94

Values of responses: none = 1, little = 2, some = 3, a lot = 4

their cultural and ethnic backgrounds, prejudice reduction training, and open forums in which students raise questions and discuss selected topics. Students who participate in the social service portion of the club, the prejudice reduction conference, and other HRC activities report gaining insight from interacting with individuals from different cultures. A continual challenge to HRC leaders is to make effective instructional use of the personal and cultural knowledge that students possess while helping them reach beyond their own cultural boundaries (Banks, 1993). Although students reported that they did learn relevant information about other cultural perspectives and traditions, they also reported a desire to learn more specific information about various cultural and religious groups.

Issue clarification

Words like racism and prejudice are complex in their meaning, and actions born out of racist or prejudicial thought have far-reaching effects. Although high school students are familiar with such phraseology, they do not necessarily fully understand the associated actions and issues, nor do they necessarily have the skills to differ-

Table 2.3. Students' perceptions of how their involvement in the HRC helped increase their knowledge of other cultural and religious groups and their ability to clarify issues of stereotyping, racism, and prejudice

| | *Percentage of Students Reporting Various Levels of Help* | | | |
Insights	*No help*	*Little help*	*Some help*	*A lot of help*
Knowledge gained regarding different cultural and religious groups	5%	10%	51%	34%
Help in clarifying issues of racism, etc.	1%	8%	32%	59%

N = 94

entiate between a racist and an opposed opinion, decision, or action. Participation in the HRC seems to help participants better clarify issues such as racism, stereotyping, and prejudice. Fifty-nine percent of the survey's respondents said that participation in the HRC helped them "a lot" in clarifying such issues, while 32 percent felt the club helped them "some" (see Table 2.3). As participants in the HRC develop an understanding of the concepts of racism, prejudice, and stereotyping, they are encouraged to reflect on their own actions and feelings and to identify stereotypes or prejudices they may have of others and the results of such perceptions. One HRC participant wrote, "The Human Relations Club has helped me to realize that I have some prejudices against certain people. Being in the club has helped me to try to change my views and to be more accepting. I know I have a ways to go but at least I am trying now."

The survey asked students to rate how their involvement in the HRC has helped them become more aware of issues such as racism, stereotyping, and prejudice in their schools, their homes, their community, and the media, and among their friends. Responses show that students' involvement in the HRC has helped them to become aware of racial and other issues in all five areas. More than 60 percent of the students reported that their participation helped them "a lot" in developing an increased awareness of instances of racism, stereotyping, and prejudice in their school, in their community, and in the media. Sixty-eight percent of the respondents reported that their HRC involvement gave them "some" or "a lot" of help in recognizing racism and prejudice among their friends (see Table 2.4).

New opportunities

Educators have known for some time that meaningful activities and experiences are effective tools in helping students internalize and process new knowledge. The HRC is designed to provide students with the opportunity to become involved and to effect change as it pertains to people understanding and accepting diversity. Essentially the HRC is geared toward helping students to develop and practice leadership skills. Besides participating in the five organized activities, members are encouraged to develop and initiate additional ways to become informed leaders in combating racism, prejudice, and stereotyping. While 40 percent of the respondents to the survey identified themselves as being involved "a lot," 69 per-

Table 2.4. Students' perceptions of how their involvement in the HRC helped to increase their awareness of issues of racism, prejudice, and stereotyping within selected areas

	Percentage of Students Reporting Various Levels of Help			
Area	*No help*	*Little help*	*Some help*	*A lot of help*
School	3%	10%	25%	62%
Home	12%	16%	32%	36%
Friends	7%	18%	34%	38%
Community	2%	8%	28%	62%
Media	2%	16%	22%	60%

N = 94

cent identified the HRC as providing "a lot" of opportunity for them to get involved.

The majority of students said that their participation in the HRC served as a catalyst for desiring to learn more about diverse groups, and that their HRC experience helped them "some" or "a lot" in developing a sense of empathy toward others subject to racism and stereotyping (see Table 2.5). Although recognition is the first step in correcting a problem, it does not necessarily mean that an individual will address the issue. Of the survey respondents, 60 percent felt that their participation in the HRC had helped them "a lot" in developing a confidence in their ability to address issues of racism, stereotyping, and prejudice, and 27 percent felt that their involvement in the club had provided "some" help in developing confidence in addressing the issues (see Table 2.5).

Students reported that they are better prepared for discussing racial issues with adults and peers, and one student said, "I always knew that it [racism] was wrong, but I never really thought about

Table 2.5. Students' perceptions of how their involvement in the HRC helped to increase their empathy toward victims of racism, prejudice, and stereotyping; their desire to learn more about other cultural, ethnic, and religious groups; and their confidence in addressing issues of racism, prejudice, and stereotyping

Identified Gains	Percentage of Students Reporting Various Levels of Help			
	No help	Little help	Some help	A lot of help
Empathy toward victims of prejudice	3%	8%	35%	54%
Desire to learn more about diverse groups	2%	12%	33%	53%
Confidence in addressing issues of prejudice	3%	10%	27%	60%

N = 94

saying anything about it until I started doing things with the Human Relations Club." HRC organizers recognize that students have daily opportunities to address multicultural issues; however, if a student is not experienced or confident in doing so, the individual may choose to ignore the issue. The HRC provides students with a support system and a format not only for becoming critical thinkers about multicultural issues but also for addressing those issues. It is the goal of the HRC that experience addressing these issues in a structured setting will result in students' willingness and ability to address them in other situations. In the future, program evaluation needs to go beyond identifying students' comfortableness in addressing issues of racism, prejudice, and stereotyping and identify specific instances of addressing such issues.

Conclusion

Multicultural education should provide experiences that lead students to value their own cultural and ethnic backgrounds and appreciate the cultures of other groups. They should value diversity as an asset in society and look for ways to encourage the richness of a pluralistic society. Schools share the responsibility of helping students acquire the knowledge and commitment needed to think, decide, and take action so that their accountability is evident in their behavior. Members of the HRC repeatedly demonstrate leadership characteristics, including vision, energy, enthusiasm, focus, and determination. Helping students to become empowered to address multicultural issues requires that students have a knowledge base, confidence, experience in addressing such issues, and a support system to facilitate and encourage their development. In this chapter I have shown how the Human Relations Club serves as a model for providing such empowerment.

The HRC creates avenues of communication and a process of dealing with often confusing issues at a practical and conscious level. The diversity of HRC activities reflects students' diverse interests and serves as a catalyst for student involvement. In the HRC, the more students are involved, the more knowledgeable and confident they become in addressing other human relations issues.

The HRC benefits not only members but the entire school system and community. It provides the initiation for elementary, middle, and secondary level students to begin discussions on multicultural issues, and it serves as a way for the school district and community to cooperatively explore issues. If students are to be prepared to live, work, and participate in a diverse society, it is necessary for them to develop a sense of their role in contributing to the well-being of that society. It is necessary for them to take a leadership role. Hamden High School's Human Relations Club accomplishes this.

References

Banks, J. *Teaching Strategies for Ethnic Studies.* Needham Heights, Mass.: Allyn & Bacon, 1984.

Banks, J. "The Cannon Debate, Knowledge Construction and Multicultural Education." *Educational Researcher*, 1993, *22*(5), 4–14.

Cohen, C. *Teaching About Ethnic Diversity.* Washington, D.C.: Office of Educational Research and Improvement, 1986. (ED 273 539)

Conrad, D., and Hedlin, D. "School-Based Community Service: What We Know from Research and Theory." *Phi Delta Kappan*, 1991, *72*(10), 743–749.

Cox, K. "Significant Adolescent Leadership Development Experiences Identified by Established Leaders in the United States." Unpublished doctoral dissertation, Department of Education, Ohio State University, 1988.

Grant, C. "Best Practices in Teacher Preparation for Urban Schools: Lessons from the Multicultural Teacher Education Literature." *Action in Teacher Education*, 1994, *21*(3), 1–18.

Lewis, B. "Today's Kids Care About Social Action." *Educational Leadership*, 1991, *49*(1) 47–49.

National Council for the Social Studies. "Curriculum Guidelines for Multicultural Education." *Social Education*, 1992, *56*(5), 274–294.

Theel, R. (ed.). "Planning for Multicultural Education at the Elementary and Middle School Levels." Syracuse, N.Y.: Syracuse City School District, 1990. (ED 330 762).

"Students and Now the High School." *Time*, February 1996, p. 8.

Webb, M. "Multicultural Education in Elementary and Secondary Schools." Washington, D.C.: Office of Educational Research and Improvement, 1990. (ED 327 613)

Willis, S. "Multicultural Teaching: Meeting the Challenges That Arise in Practice." *Association for Supervision and Curriculum Development Curriculum Update*, 1993, p. 1.

Willison, S. "When Students Volunteer to Feed the Hungry: Some Considerations for Educators." *The Social Studies*, 1994, *85*(2), 88–90.

Woyach, R. *Preparing For Leadership: A Young Adult's Guide to Leadership Skills in a Global Age*. Westport, Conn.: Greenwood Press, 1992.

SCOTT WILLISON *is associate professor at Boise State University and was the administrative liaison to the Hamden High School Human Relations Club.*

This chapter describes one high school's reform effort that led to the establishment of the Student Leadership Institute. The mission of the institute is to identify and develop positive leadership potential among members of the student body. The school has literally turned around, with demonstrable growth in all areas. The empowerment of students to intervene in their own learning environment has been a phenomenal success.

3

The Student Leadership Institute

R. E. Daniel

CLARE MARIE WEDDLE IS WELL INTO a typically busy day. Her application for Harvard early decision is due to be postmarked today and she needs the principal's letter of recommendation before she mails it. Typically, she is handling this detail between A.P. European History and A.P. English, heading for the school's main office while intensely trading review questions with a couple of her classmates for a calculus test this afternoon—right after physics.

Clare enters the main office, frustrated but not surprised to find that I am not on campus at the time (I hardly ever am when she needs something from me, or so she says). So she catches my secretary coming out of the copier room and asks to be let into my private office while her friends scurry on to class, still furiously quizzing each other. My secretary lets Clare in without hesitation, knowing that I have entrusted her with a wide variety of specific assignments, and she goes through the stacks on my desk until she finds the recommendation letter. Taking this opportunity to get some of those critical assignments done, she seats herself at my desk

NEW DIRECTIONS FOR SCHOOL LEADERSHIP, NO. 4, SUMMER 1997 © JOSSEY-BASS PUBLISHERS

and, utilizing my personal long-distance line, makes three quick phone calls to the superintendent's secretary, a county commissioner, and the regional director of a local band. Her conversation with each is cordial and familiar. Her business completed, she lets herself out, locking the door behind her.

Now Clare is a few minutes late to English class, so she requests a hall pass from the receptionist, who gives it to her without questioning her need for it. In the hall, she passes an assistant principal who has stopped three other students to check their passes. Clare waves her pass and continues on; the assistant principal is satisfied with the legality of her passage. It has been his experience that this particular student is in the hall for a legitimate purpose having to do with school business, or she would not be in the hall.

On the way to her English class Clare stops in two other classrooms to deliver thank-yous to faculty and staff members for their recent involvement in a student-led project. She reaches her class and takes her seat just in time to answer a question directed at her. She fields it easily. The teacher is not surprised, for it is not uncommon for this particular student to arrive a few minutes late, nor is it uncommon for her to be able to handle the questions leveled at her "on the fly." She is, after all, one of the school's premier student leaders.

School culture that supports student leadership

How much is it worth to have a school culture that is characterized by participation by the leaders of the student body, acting in concert with the faculty, staff, and administration to pursue common goals for the good of the entire community? How many schools have students like Clare, who has earned the level of trust necessary to allow her such unusual access to faculty, staff, administration, and resources, all on her own recognizance? It is important to note that Clare moves about the school and handles her responsibilities well within the established rules and regulations—she is not exempt, for instance, from the requirement to have a hall pass while in the hall after class time begins. This is not an example of unusual privilege; it is an example of how a student who exhibits the highest possible potential for leadership can find herself in a position of trust and respect unparalleled in a typical school culture.

The secretary lets Clare into the office because I, the principal, have demonstrated my trust in her to get certain things done. She has earned the right to handle things that I would otherwise have to handle myself, and so she has access to my office, phone, copier code, and other resources that make it possible to get our mutual business done. The assistant principal knows that when Clare "waves" a piece of paper at him in the hall it is a legitimate hall pass. And the English teacher knows that Clare would not be allowed to continue in this position of trust and responsibility if she did not also keep up her classroom obligations, so she is confident that when Clare makes it to class she will be prepared.

Clare Marie Weddle, who is the highest-ranked member of her class, also owns a unique distinction at Reidsville High School (RHS): she is president of the RHS Student Leadership Institute (SLI). Along with a larger group of similarly minded and highly motivated students she has completed the most demanding program available to aspiring leaders the school has to offer. She routinely demonstrates a level of commitment above and beyond that expected of students. Now it is her job to oversee the training of other students in the way she was trained, personally fulfilling the SLI's mission "to identify and develop positive leadership potential among members of the RHS student body."

History of the SLI

The RHS Student Leadership Institute was developed as a direct response to a critical need for student ownership in the school. At one time, RHS was the crown jewel of the Reidsville school system, one of four school systems in Rockingham County, North Carolina. The chief benefactor of the school system and the city was American Tobacco Company, which had supported the local economy for so long that its announced sale and imminent closing early in the 1990s stunned a community that had come to think of itself as insulated from economic problems. In addition, for years a growing problem of "white flight" to schools just outside the city had slowly tipped the school's racial balance to create a fifty-fifty black-white mix in a town that was predominately white. So this school found itself to be an object of tension and dissatisfaction within its own community, forced to spend more and more time and resources battling a growing perception of inferiority that was unfounded but almost impossible to fight. When the Reidsville City School Board finally called it quits and turned their charter over to the Rockingham County commissioners in 1991, effectively forcing a merger between the city and county schools, the commissioners responded by forcing the other two city systems to join in the merger as well. Reidsville therefore became the pariah of the county, having "taken our schools away."

I came to Reidsville in the middle of the mess, assuming the principalship of Reidsville High School at a time when the students, faculty, and staff were facing problems of growing racial tension, declining student performance scores, and defensive public relations. As the only high school in the county with a significant minority population (the other three high school populations are approximately 21 percent, 17 percent, and 9 percent minority, while RHS is very nearly 50 percent black and 50 percent white), RHS also fought a constant and ugly propaganda war. Families moving into the area were routinely told outrageous horror stories about guns, knives, roving gangs of out-of-control African American youth, and corridor drug deals. Not surprisingly, these rumors resulted in even more ill feeling in the school and community. To make matters worse, the merger was only one year away, and the Reidsville City Schools superintendent who had presided over the forced merger, and during the announced death of American Tobacco Company, got out while he could, leaving his assistant superintendent in the position of caretaker for the year remaining before the Reidsville City Schools were no more.

I stepped into the open principalship at RHS fresh from my first principalship on the other side of the state. I had been in the job a

full three months before I found out that not one certified administrator in Rockingham County had even applied for the job,
including the three RHS assistant principals and an entire contingent of teachers certified in administration and waiting for their
"break."

From the outset, it was obvious that the student body felt disenfranchised by the school, the school system, the faculty and staff,
and the school administration. In a series of conversations with volunteer students called the "Principal's Roundtable," I was bombarded with bitterness and frustration from the students as well as
with a multitude of ideas for correcting some things about which
they felt strongly. As the students saw more and more evidence that
they were being listened to, the more motivated ones began gravitating toward involvement with the new order of things, and it
became clear that many RHS students were strong and capable, just
like students in every American high school, and were willing to
put themselves on the line in favor of a cause in which they
believed. So, building on an idea generated by the students themselves, of putting students in leadership and decision-making positions with real input and influence over school policy and practices,
the Student Leadership Institute (SLI) was born.

At the time I had only a general idea of what we were trying to
accomplish and how to go about it. Having been director of an
award-winning marching band program for many years before
moving into administration, I was comfortable in the actual process
of spotting leadership potential and nursing it along, building character and strength in students so that they were capable of extraordinary feats of peer motivation and supervision. But exactly how
to translate that process into a schoolwide program dealing with
nonspecific problems of culture and attitude was nearly inconceivable. What "charge" was I to put to SLI? Somehow "Go forth and
rid this school of bad attitude" did not seem reasonable.

In developing the initial idea into a full-grown program, I
enlisted the help of two teachers; one veteran and one enthusiastic
youngster. We decided early on to concentrate on actual leadership
practice and look past the obvious school-centered indicators that
so often define all school endeavors. After all, sometimes the "true"

leaders are not the ones we wish they would be; often students pick their own leaders for reasons other than strong character, a high sense of honor, or super achievement. So, for us there was no minimum grade average, no specific attendance or performance criteria, no teacher recommendations, no grade-level quota. We opened SLI up to any student who nominated himself or herself and was willing to commit to the training. Several students jumped at the chance immediately, and others we recruited. When we opened the first weekend training retreat, forty-one students were in attendance, including several athletes, a few elected student leaders, a handful of honor-roll students, some brash and cheeky class clowns, a couple of geeky nerds, some beauty queen cheerleaders, and some pregrunge longhairs. The group was predominately female (and has remained so throughout SLI's history) and predominately white (this has changed so that SLI is now more reflective of the fifty-fifty school population, and has been for two out of five years). Nearly every type of student was represented in the first group, and that continues to be so to this day. This is a particular point of pride for SLI because of its commitment to meritocracy and diversity; we began with an emphasis on cutting across racial, cultural, gender, religious, scholastic, and economic barriers among students, and that emphasis endures.

SLI training and programs

The SLI training process was modeled after the newly emerging civic leadership training programs that were popping up around the state and country, programs with names like Leadership Charlotte and the Humberg Jaycees' Civic Leadership Forum, in which aspiring civic and business leaders go through a four- to six-month training regimen, spending one or two days each month in seminars and workshops designed to introduce them to their city or county and its unique economic, structural, political, historical, geographical, and educational challenges. In addition to offering field trips to see elected and appointed leaders in action—the city

council, the county commissioners, the school board, and the state's
general assembly—SLI initially sought to bring specific issues into
focus for its members through its own innovative programs. The
Race Relations Forum, the Business and Civic Leaders' Forum, the
RHS Graduates' Forum, and Law and Youth Day are open events
in which community, civic, legal, and business leaders from the
community are brought into the school to face a curious and sometimes frighteningly straightforward group of determined teenagers
who are not a bit shy about posing the tough questions. These
events are part of the training regimen for every class of "Candidates," and they are planned and implemented by SLI "Actives"—
members who have completed the initial training and now train the
new Candidates. Over the last five years these events have taken on
somewhat of a life of their own. This year's Race Relations Forum,
for example, attracted the attention of at least two out-of-town TV
news departments as well as two principals from other schools. Perhaps it helped that last year's forum featured a shouting match
between one of our panelists, a local businessman, and one of our
audience guests, a city councilman, who disagreed strongly on a
matter of community concern that was then polarizing the town
along racial lines. The students who were in leadership training and
who asked the tough questions leading up to the argument were
thoroughly disgusted with these adults, having learned in SLI to
handle disagreements agreeably.

The very first group of SLI students took on, as its first project,
the enormous challenge of improving race relations at RHS. This
was remarkable for several reasons. First, race relations were
admittedly tense, with the very real chance of eruptions every day.
Second, there was no clear mandate among the student body at
large for dealing with the issue; SLI was going it alone in this, recognizing that they might have to stand alone and face down their
friends. Third, the group was predominantly white, with no historical precedent for this type of activity. And fourth, no one had
a clue how to guide the students in this, and they knew it. We,
the adult advisors, were enthusiastic but helpless as to what to
tell them.

As you might expect, the students rose to the occasion brilliantly, without our help except in "greasing the skids" for logistical support. On their own, they commissioned a racial harmony mural for the central commons from one of the art department's most accomplished student artists. (Here is where having the principal himself as chief advisor really helped—they were able to cut through most of the red tape surrounding most student organizations' on-campus efforts.) Totally on their own they began meeting together in mixed racial groups to visit one another's churches on Sunday mornings. This really did cause apoplexy in certain parts of the community during the month or two when this group of students first showed up together at area churches, but it was quickly and smoothly accepted and integrated into a fledgling movement to institute community-wide black-white special services several times each year. SLI thus found itself on the cutting edge of a new partnership project in the community that served its own and the community's broader interests very nicely. And in a final gesture of bravery and cooperation, they began to deliberately hang out together, crossing the last barrier of institutionalized racism among the students themselves and daring others to follow their example. Within the first school year of this experiment, there was no longer a "white side" and a "black side" to the cafeteria, and the two-page senior class yearbook portrait in SLI's second year no longer divided itself along the spine of the book by students' color.

As important as good race relations were, and as desperately as they were needed, they were not the only area in which SLI had an effect. In concert with other schoolwide reforms being enacted by the faculty in the area of teaching methodology and assessment procedures, SLI took the lead among students in publicly emphasizing a need for the reestablishment of a tradition of scholarship among the students most capable of leading in that area. While our top students always held their own on SAT and state test scores in comparison with the students in the other county high schools, the fact that we had such a larger pool of disadvantaged and economically challenged students guaranteed that our average scores would always be lower. The leading scholars among the SLI Actives and the later Candidates resolved to intervene positively in the classroom environments themselves, exerting positive leadership through volunteer tutoring, frequent exhortation and admonition of their peers in a positive manner ("academic cheerleading"), and a specific effort to back up the teacher in establishing an enthusiastic atmosphere for learning. SLI's influence and determination brought this focus on academics to the attention of the student body. As a result, our average test scores have stopped their downward spiral and stabilized, and are even beginning to rise significantly in some areas as the school brings itself back to its feet. It must be noted here that a great many projects, most notably a radical overhaul of the approach to teaching itself, figured in this effort; the most important thing to note is that SLI took the lead in bringing the student body "on-line" so that the schoolwide reform effort was truly cooperative, involving both faculty and students.

In one of the most dramatic stories of SLI's work, the public image of the school began to be healed and changed by virtue of the determined efforts of this group of students who took the initiative to "talk up" their school. One of SLI's specific goals was the spreading of the good news about RHS, and they took every opportunity to engage in that activity. SLI Actives spoke at area elementary schools, shushed their peers who put down the school in public, and did not hesitate to confront anyone they heard badmouthing the school in the community. As principal, I used what clout I could muster to sustain a biweekly newspaper column in which I trumpeted the same thing. The result: we began to hear a change in attitude around the community, and many people seemed truly relieved that they could once again speak well of a school they used to treasure but had been forced to keep quiet about for fear of public ridicule. For the first time in years, the community began to hear what was good about Reidsville High School instead of what was bad. The mood in the town has changed so much that RHS people—students and parents alike—are no longer afraid to

challenge people they overhear in the grocery line and other public places who are spreading damaging falsehoods about the school
(a prevalent practice until recently).

SLI involvement and student character

Over the last five years, SLI has grown from a small group of students willing to buck the tide of tradition into a well-organized
group of conscientious students who take their role very seriously.
In addition to giving up numerous hours in seminars, forums, field
trips, retreats, and study sessions, they demand the highest level of
behavior from themselves. During the second year of my tenure
here, the SLI students engineered a complete overhaul of the
school's student council, lobbying for and achieving permission to
rewrite the constitution and bylaws and turning the organization
into the truly representative Student Government Association
(SGA) with real power to influence school operations. Again, having the principal as the chief advisor for the SGA made this process
very smooth and easy. While not all SGA member are SLI members, all SLI Actives are automatically SGA members, and many of
them also hold SGA offices. The SGA therefore includes a healthy
mix of students who have earned their way into the corridors of
decision making by virtue of their status as Actives in SLI, and students who are voted in during a popularity-contest vote. The SGA
president, who is elected by the student body, is still the highest-
ranking student in the school, but the SLI president ranks second,
and both sit on the Student Advisory Council, which meets
monthly with me.

The training process for SLI Candidates can be described as part
school, part community, part business, and part fraternity. Candidates are chosen strictly by self-nomination, and every RHS student, regardless of academic or behavioral background, is
encouraged to attempt SLI training. Unexcused absence from any
training event is automatically grounds for dismissal from the Candidates class, and excuses are given only for very specific and invi-

olate reasons: personal illness; death in the immediate family; prior commitment to a school function, such as organized school athletics; and emergency family situations that demand the student's presence (students must be excused in advance for this one at the request of the parents directly to the student's SLI advisor). Any disciplinary infraction resulting in in-school suspension (ISS) or worse also results in dismissal from the Candidates class. Once a student has been installed as an SLI Active, he or she is expected to be an example of applied leadership to the rest of the student body. The SLI Actives police their own ranks, and any disciplinary infraction that results in ISS or worse is dealt with by a specially convened peer review board that decides what shall be done in addition to the actual disciplinary action taken by the school administration, in accordance with the severity of the infraction and its impact on the reputation of the school and of SLI. It is remarkable to note that in its five-year history, no more than a dozen or so SLI Actives have ever been involved in a disciplinary infraction.

Even in the best of programs, there will always be a few people who fall short of the program's expectations. SLI is no exception, and that is the area in which the organization's chief advisor must be very sensitive in his or her relationships with the school's faculty. From the outset, the members of the SLI were considered "the principal's pets" by a few hardheaded faculty and staff members who also derided every other reform and change instituted at the school. I anticipated this response and built an expectation of it and a method of dealing with it into training sessions. The first group especially had it hard: at least a dozen of them had had run-ins with various faculty and staff members over one issue or another prior to becoming SLI Candidates. It was vital to show that SLI training and participation could and would change these students' attitudes so that they could overcome this history with the faculty and staff. As the program has grown and become accepted and honored within the school community, it has taken on some of the baggage that goes with being the best—namely, it attracts more and more potential Candidates for the wrong reasons, and weeding out such candidates becomes more and more difficult. It is truly now a point of pride at RHS to be an SLI Active, and some students will go into training simply to be able to say they are SLI members. Overall, however, the students themselves do a very effective job of holding the new Candidates accountable for their actions. After all, to become an SLI Active you have had to prove that you are capable of commitment, sacrifice, teamwork, and leadership. Those characteristics do not come easily, and the students who achieve that status are not eager to share their accomplishments with students who will not properly appreciate their efforts.

As chief advisor, I have seen the beginning of the realization of my greatest dreams for this group: they are truly the leaders of the school's culture. Of course, we still have an occasional tense moment in race relations—any American high school, especially one in the South with a fifty-fifty racial mix is bound to. But it is no longer something that we in the administration fear, because we know we can work it through and that SLI will do its part to defuse the inevitable surrounding student tension. Once in a while, a high-ranking SLI Active will go slightly astray and become a normal teenage kid, with all the foibles and frustrations that go with American youthdom. When that happens to an SLI Active, however, the entire faculty and staff is more inclined to give the student the benefit of the doubt in light of the student's previously demonstrated leadership capabilities. And when the campus gets overly dirty, or a particularly nasty rumor gets started, SLI can be counted on to pull itself up and take command, bringing to bear all the leadership skills and applying all the training at their command. And if you have never seen highly trained and highly motivated determined teenagers tackle a problem with no thought of defeat, you have never seen one of the most beautiful and inspiring sights an educator can ever see. For these are truly the citizens under whose leadership you and I will pass the torch of power and civilization to a new generation. I for one can pass that torch knowing that at least a few RHS students are prepared to take it and run the good race for a far, far greater distance than they would have been able to go otherwise.

Advice for principals

I strongly urge school principals who are considering starting an SLI-type organization to consider the following points of advice:

Be serious. Kids are notoriously adept at spotting phoniness, especially among adults in authority. They will not give you the time of day if you do not mean it when you pitch it to them.

Recognize the kids' right to ownership. No organization or effort aimed at empowering teenagers can survive if the terms of its survival are dictated to the participants. They must take charge of the effort themselves, and they must be allowed to take it in the direction they see fit.

Back them up. Your effort is doomed to failure from the get go if the students do not have the authority to effect real change. This is a powerful argument for having the principal act as the chief advisor, because no administrative doublespeak or fabricated political barriers can stand in the principal's way. And the school faculty, staff, and administration absolutely *must* be willing to give students the opportunity to try and to fail without crushing their enthusiasm.

Expect the students to rise to the occasion. The illustration I used at the beginning of this chapter is every bit true: the SLI president has unlimited access to the resources and privileges that go along with true leadership. Clare Marie Weddle, this year's RHS SLI president, is accepted by the entire school staff in her capacity as a leader with legitimate business to conduct, and she has earned the right to come and go, even to use my office and work at my desk, as she deems necessary. She even knows my personal copier code and makes use of my telephone line. I will not put her in the position of being responsible for a $10,000 master key to the campus, but my office staff has instructions to let her into wherever she needs to go, whenever she needs to go there.

Maintain high standards. SLI Actives are expected to exhibit constant leadership behavior in the classroom, in the cafeteria, on the grounds, and in the community. They have been trained in the subtle art of peer pressure manipulation, and they exercise it in keeping the lunch lines skip-free, the campus cleaner than it would be otherwise, and the community gossip machine in check. We do not impose on them the burden of being "student administrators"—they are not required to be "rats" or informers against their peers; I will not allow them to become a principal's secret spy network. Instead, I insist that they exercise their own leadership judgment and put a stop on the spot to any behavior that is detrimental to the school and to their own learning environment. This approach is actually much more effective than running to tell me, anyway, because it occurs immediately and utilizes the enormous power of peer influence.

Trust them. Having invested enormous amounts of time and energy to get my Actives trained, I have found it to be in the best interest of the school to trust them, even when I am suspicious of their motivation or scared of possible negative outcomes. This is where it becomes necessary to know the difference between "advisor" and "leader." The students choose their own leaders; I am chief advisor. While the line occasionally gets blurred, the two roles work surprisingly well as separate functions.

Give no slack. As much as it hurts, when an SLI student goes off the deep end, forgets his or her training, and becomes a normal teenager, putting himself or herself in the position of hurting the whole group by dint of his or her behavior, I must take action. If I do not, the entire operation will lose all respect from the faculty and staff. SLI students must believe me when I tell them that they will *not* be accorded any extra slack. Indeed, just the opposite is true. I specifically train them to recognize that the world is not fair, that it never will be, and that their leadership effectiveness depends directly upon how well they exercise that leadership even in the face of injustice and unfairness, more so than on how they handle it when all is going well. Consequently, my SLI students are well aware that I hold them responsible at a higher level than I hold most other students. An infraction that would earn a typical student a simple reprimand or an after-school RAM service (campus cleanup detail) can and often does earn the SLI student a much more severe punishment. What is more, I require that these students demonstrate their understanding of that punishment and verbally accept it in order to remain Active. So, when I must take action I do so swiftly and publicly, making sure that no one can ever say that "Johnny" got away with anything simply because he is SLI.

Hold no prejudice. This is especially important in the area of scholastics. The plain fact of the matter is that some of the most serious and effective student leaders may simply not be the most outstanding scholars. Be willing to recognize student leadership potential among the *whole* student body, and nurture it.

Keep on keepin' on. Finally, understand that this project is ongoing and must be constantly attended to. After all, every four years we get a completely new group of students, many of whom have never before heard of SLI or the reasons for it.

Here's wishing you as much success as we have had here at North Carolina's finest high school!

R. E. DANIEL *is currently the principal of Reidsville High School, Reidsville, North Carolina.*

*Urban high schools are increasingly struggling with the ques-
tion of how to turn students into leaders. The High School for
Leadership and Public Service, a magnet high school in Manhattan, New York, and Syracuse University's Maxwell School
of Public Affairs and Citizenship have developed a leadership
curriculum for freshmen. The high school uses real-life documents (such as the Constitution) and situations (such as lobbying in the political arena) to teach leadership.*

4

Setting an example worth following: The challenge of teaching leadership

Heather H. Ordover

THE HIGH SCHOOL FOR LEADERSHIP AND PUBLIC SERVICE (HSLAPS),
a New York City public school, was founded in 1993. Its motto is
"Leadership means setting an example worth following." The
school is part of a districtwide program called *New Visions*. One of
the purposes of New Visions is to pair small schools with corporate
or academic sponsors. HSLAPS's partner is Syracuse University's
Maxwell School of Citizenship and Public Affairs. The Maxwell
School provides the HSLAPS with alumni tutors, student interns,
faculty advisors, and money for leadership curriculum development.
The training that HSLAPS's teachers have received has been initiated and provided by the university.

The first challenge HSLAPS encountered as part of New
Visions was to develop a curriculum that included leadership devel-
opment and prepared students to pass the New York State Board
Exams (a prerequisite to graduation). After much debate, it was

NEW DIRECTIONS FOR SCHOOL LEADERSHIP, NO. 4, SUMMER 1997 © JOSSEY-BASS PUBLISHERS

decided that a separate class would be created for freshmen that allowed the students to build their leadership skills by learning about public policy and public service while working on their writing. One academic period four times a week would be used as the school's leadership class for freshmen to address policy work; sophomore leadership classes would incorporate computer literacy and ethics; juniors would take law classes; and seniors would take a class called Participation in Government and Virtual Enterprise.

HSLAPS and Syracuse University define leadership as the ability to use organization, persuasion, and example to motivate a group to pursue goals shared by the leader and the group. Students study leadership themes such as public policy and public service. Public policy is rules set by governing bodies for the public welfare. The study of public policy is the study of the processes of policy creation and the skills needed to create and influence policy.

William D. Coplin, professor of public affairs at the Maxwell School of Public Affairs and Citizenship, is our primary contact. Not only has Coplin been intimately involved in the founding and planning of HSLAPS, but his entire staff has been involved with the birth of the school. His textbooks and his students who serve as our interns have been invaluable to our process.

HSLAPS has relied on Coplin's definition of leadership in shaping our freshman curriculum. He sees leadership as a complex set of skills, knowledge, attitudes, and personal characteristics. He writes:

Effective leaders are individuals who have solid academic, problem-solving, and interpersonal skills, have a vision about improving society, and have the initiative and persistence to pursue that vision. In any given leadership situation, such leaders must have detailed knowledge of the context, and the analytical ability to identify problems and causes and to develop solutions that are both effective and politically feasible. They must also be able to build consensus among supporters as well as negotiate with key stakeholders. Finally, they must want to improve conditions and must be willing to make the necessary commitment in time and effort to lead others to do what they can to achieve a better world. The role of education is to provide an environment in which life-changing experiences can occur. Given the characteristics of leadership listed above, that environment must begin with the basic interests and knowledge of the students and push the student to develop academic, problem-solving, and interpersonal skills; create a vision that would solve a serious policy problem; and learn how initiative and persistence is acquired [letter to the author, February 20, 1997].

The main thrust of our academic curriculum is in writing. As educators, we know that students do better when we have high expectations, give them "real" work, and show them their need for what they are learning. If we give them form without substance they will not see the usefulness of it and will disengage from the class. All of the freshmen writing activities, therefore, focus on problem solving and examinations of cause and effect in real-world issues. This style of writing is not easy, and it takes them some time to acquire the skills they need. For a class like this, an unlimited rewrite option is extremely useful. Because we use a writing rubric based on attaining levels of competency, the students are not threatened by the punishment of bad grades. The papers they produce are more creative because they are willing to go out on a limb and try new styles and ideas. Students learn to write persuasively and to use sources to back up their ideas and increase their authority. The biggest benefit I find to this philosophy in a leadership setting is the behavior it reinforces: if you just keep trying, eventually you will succeed.

Leadership class 1996–97

At Coplin's urging, we began this school year studying constitutions. Coplin encouraged the students to write a classroom constitution of their own to insure that there was a common framework and understanding of how decisions should be made in the classroom. I realized that my students had only a vague idea of our country's Constitution and no idea of why anyone would actually want one. One student in the early weeks said, "It's just a bunch of rules telling you what not to do. It's stupid. I hate it." Noting this, I decided that our best bet might be to read and dissect two constitutions: our own, and that of the Iroquois (a northeastern Native American tribe).

The theoretical implications of the two very different documents we read at the start of the year are enormous, and these documents provided us with good fodder for discussion as well as two immediate models to work from. The Iroquois constitution, which lasted for about four hundred years, peacefully brought together five often-warring northeastern Native American tribes: the Mohawk, Oneida, Seneca, Cayuga, and Onondaga. The students were perplexed by a document called a constitution that appeared to contain no laws and no punishment system. Upon closer examination, they realized that the document was largely a metaphor for how to live a peaceful life. It appears that the worst punishment one could suffer within this tribal society was to lose the respect of one's people. This is a striking contrast to our very literal system of checks and balances, punishments and penalties. Having both constitutions at our fingertips provided us with a base for discussion of how we wanted our room to be run, how we wanted to see our world run, and what kind of leaders each constitution created or denied.

Our next step turned out to be the real-life task of improving the school's fire drill procedure. What appeared at the outset to be a week-and-a-half workshop grew to be a three-week processing of ideas and arguments. The students were given a real problem to solve that affected them directly. They took strong ownership of the process, knowing that if they did well their policy would be implemented and they would be able to take credit for making their school better. During one heated discussion, I stopped the class and reminded them that they were fighting over fire bells. Nervous laughter could not hide the light bulbs that went off over all heads—including mine. We were not debating hot-button issues— health care or welfare reform—we were simply trying to find out if there might be a more efficient way to move five hundred students out of a fourteen-story office building and onto a busy Manhattan street using only two staircases. One student finally said, "So this is why it takes Congress so long to get things done?" Our constitutional complainer became the most rabid defender of the class fire drill policy, often saying, "But if everyone would just *think* about why we need these rules, they would follow the rules! They just need to sit down and discuss the issues!" Real-life problems turned my classroom into a minicongress of fully engaged thinkers.

With the written policy now complete, the next step in the process is for the students to present the policy proposal to the school, to see if they can get the policy adopted. Lobbying, too, is an important part of leadership in the real world.

Leadership tomorrow

Must every school have a separate leadership class to teach the qualities of leadership? Probably not. Aspects of leadership can certainly be studied in other classes. If a leader is defined as a risk taker who can rally the troops to get things done, then an immediate question should follow: How do we want that leader to get things done? That decision is made implicitly by each teacher in how she presents herself to the class. We must always take the high road in a leadership setting and model the behavior we want to see. We know all too well that the current media that bombards these young minds often tells the students the exact opposite of what they will learn in a leadership class. The truth is that nothing good comes easy, you have to work for what you want, and luck tends to come only when you are properly prepared. We, the teachers, have to decide to be good leaders first; then we can implement a leadership curriculum. We cannot ask students to look to our current scandal-plagued Congress or to the equally problematic White House; we cannot always rely on parents to demonstrate the qualities of a leader. Ultimately, HSLAPS has discovered, if teachers are to be the professionals in charge of the vital task of drawing out of tomorrow's leaders the skills they will need to lead, we must first be leaders ourselves. As one of my freshmen students said, "We are not born leaders, we must be guided to become leaders."

HEATHER H. ORDOVER is currently teaching at the High School for Leadership and Public Service in Manhattan, New York.

Although students are often the beneficiaries of restructuring efforts in schools, they are rarely consulted about what or how to change. In this chapter we argue that students can make a positive contribution to change efforts and that their involvement is consistent with constructivist goals of restructuring. We also report initial findings from an ongoing study of an urban high school that has included students as partners in restructuring. These initial findings support our argument that students not only have valuable ideas to contribute, but can also take an active leadership role when given the opportunity.

5

We have ideas: Students' voices in restructuring

Cynthia J. Reed, David Bechtel

No problem can be solved from the same consciousness that created it.

—Albert Einstein

RESTRUCTURING IS ON THE REFORM AGENDA for schools across the country. Although the term is difficult to define precisely, it conveys the idea that schools need to be changed in systemic, fundamental ways in order to move from a factory-oriented style of schooling to one that is intended to develop life skills in students to prepare them for our changing world.

Note: We would like to thank the other members of the Documentation Team for their assistance in conducting and analyzing this study: William Bickel, Marie Connors-Gilmore, De Voka Gordon, and Tonikiaa Orange.

NEW DIRECTIONS FOR SCHOOL LEADERSHIP, NO. 4, SUMMER 1997 © JOSSEY-BASS PUBLISHERS

The restructuring movement can be seen to encompass three strands: changing the structure of schooling, changing roles and responsibilities, and changing the culture of schools. Suggested structural changes include decentralization, shared decision making, flexible scheduling, teacher teaming, and school choice (Newmann and Wehlage, 1995). Proponents argue that restructuring schools means that all members of the school community must reevaluate their present roles and responsibilities as well as their basic assumptions about the purpose of education. There needs to be a move away from emphasizing the hierarchical relationships that currently exist and toward an emerging concept of valuing the opinions and ideas of all members of the school community (Fullan and Miles, 1992). Over the past decade there has been a move toward increased collaboration with stakeholders in public education—parents, community members, administration, and teachers—but students have rarely been included. "When adults do think of students, they think of them as potential beneficiaries of change. They think of achievement results, skills, attitudes, and jobs. They rarely think of students as participants in a process of change and organizational life" (Fullan and Miles, 1992, p. 751).

Involving students in the restructuring process

If a purpose of the reform effort is truly to attempt to break away from hierarchical relationships, then involving students throughout the reform initiative is one way to demonstrate that adults are serious about change efforts. By involving students in restructuring, schools get fresh and different perspectives on the process of improving schools. Students are keenly aware of what works for their learning and what does not. They can offer many insights about possible changes in the schooling system. Students can help reformers to solve the "right" problem by expressing their unique points of view. "In the area of education, complex problems cannot be broken down into simple elements without running [into] the problem of producing the right solution to the wrong problem" (Dunn, Basom, and Frantz, 1988, p. 24).

Villa and Thousand (1995) identify three additional reasons for involving students in collaborative research roles with adults, which can be extrapolated to involving students in restructuring. First, because educational reform efforts suggest that students need to exercise high-level thinking skills to contribute to their learning, restructuring provides opportunities to exercise those skills. Second, collaborating with adults about learning helps students to "develop the ethic and practice of contributing to and caring for a greater community and society" (p. 104). Third, teaming is the most effective way to survive the information explosion we continue to undergo. By modeling collaboration, shared decision making, and instructional power, educators can help students to develop the teaming skills that are needed in today's society.

By engaging students in the restructuring process, we are signaling to them that their ideas are important. If the purpose of schooling is to encourage thinking about learning, then involving students in discussions about school reorganization works toward accomplishing that goal. In Nieto's (1994) study, many students were likely to be disengaged from their learning, at least initially. By entering into discussions about what to change, students began to consider what aspects of their learning they valued most, and they offered insights about why curricula were irrelevant or culturally offensive. The process helped to illuminate the policies and practices that cause roadblocks for many students.

Participatory planning encourages individuals' ownership of the coming changes in schools, and it helps people to prepare for those changes by getting them to believe that change really will occur. Students need time to prepare for and make sense of the impending changes by having time for discussion and reflection about them. Unless students have some meaningful role in the enterprise, most educational change—indeed, most education—will fail. I ask the reader not to think of students as running the school but to entertain the following question: What would happen if we treated the student as someone whose opinion mattered in the introduction and implementation of reform in schools (Fullan, 1991, p. 170)?

Background for our study

Since May 1995, we have been documenting change efforts at a large urban high school. Although the school has experienced problems in recent years, including racial and gang tensions, it was recently named one of 266 Blue Ribbon Schools by the U.S. Department of Education, and more than 90 percent of its students consistently attend college after graduation. Even so, there is the perception among some students that this school is actually three schools corresponding to the three tracked levels of course offerings: coursework for the gifted, college preparatory courses, and traditional program courses. As in any school, there is room for improvement.

In the summer of 1995, a three-year restructuring effort was begun with the assistance of a local foundation. The goal of this effort is to make the school mission of "preparing all students to become thinking, responsive, productive, and caring citizens" a reality. Members of the school community, including parents, other representatives of the community, teachers, administrators, and students, have joined together in what they have called "the Partnership." The Partnership members have been involved in ongoing problem solving and planning efforts to move the school closer toward achieving its mission. Particular emphasis has been paid to including students' voices in the restructuring process. Students are prominent members of the Partnership and are drawn from all three instructional programs as well as from various student leadership groups within the school, such as the principal's advisory committee, student government, and Hands Across the Campus, a group that fosters respect for diversity. A few of the student participants are former gang members. Thus far, planning activities have included a two-day retreat, subsequent planning meetings, visits to other innovative schools, staff development sessions, and discussions about moving toward alternate (block) scheduling.

As part of a larger documentation effort, we conducted two focus groups with eight of the thirteen student leaders who have actively participated in the Partnership so far. The focus groups concentrated on the students' role in the restructuring effort and produced information relevant to arguments for including students in restructuring.

We asked the students four key questions in the focus groups: (1) In what ways do you feel you have a voice in restructuring efforts at your school? (2) In what ways do you feel your voices are heard? (3) In what ways do you believe your voices make a difference? and (4) How might any barriers to the communication of your ideas be overcome? Although our study looked quite broadly at students' roles in restructuring, this chapter reports results directly related to the impact of including students' voices in restructuring.

Our approach to collecting data

We conducted two focus groups with student leaders who have been active in the initial planning phase of restructuring at their school. A prepared script of ground rules and guiding questions was used with each focus group. Each group had one facilitator and one recorder. Additionally, each group was audiotaped so that we could verify the accuracy of our field notes. We identified themes from the focus groups using two methods of analysis. One researcher coded and analyzed both sets of field notes. Another researcher identified themes by listening to and coding responses on the audiotapes. The research team reviewed both the notes and the tapes, as well as the two analyses, and through discussion reached a consensus on the major themes of the focus groups.

Preliminary findings

We developed five main themes from our analysis of the student leader focus groups.

Theme one: Students have a vision for restructuring

The students involved in the study were united in their vision of restructuring for their school. The primary purpose, in their eyes, is to improve communication and understanding for each of the partnership groups: parents, community members, teachers, and students. One student noted the importance of improving communication: "They use the word 'partnership' a lot. They try to make us feel like we're partners." Another student summarized the purpose of restructuring: "To bring the school together, find out where we can solve problems."

Theme two: Students have a sophisticated view of the change process, but feel frustrated

Some of the students evinced a sophisticated conception of the change process. Many understood that significant changes in the school will take time and require much work. In discussing the need for teachers to use new instructional methods, one student noted: "It's a scary thing for teachers. It requires a lot of work for teachers to change, and change is scary." Another student argued that planning was important. He suggested that his subcommittee make two site visits, "one to a private school, one to a public school, to get ideas—see stuff that is achievable."

Other students expressed frustration over the lack of action. They felt that planning is important, but so is action. As one student noted, "We put all these good ideas on large pieces of paper and they get stuck in an office somewhere. We should stop coming up with all these ideas and just stick with one."

Theme three: Students see barriers to change

The student leaders identified numerous barriers to change. As mentioned earlier, some of the students noted a general fear of change. Others cited the lack of accurate information among students not involved in the Partnership as a major problem, especially in relation to potential changes like block scheduling. As one student noted, "A lot of students are talking [about block scheduling], but there is a huge problem. No one ever talked to them about it." As noted earlier, the students saw the focus on planning rather than on action as a potential barrier. Pent-up feelings of frustration and individual agendas on the part of Partnership members were also identified as barriers. Students suggested that other students besides the main student leaders should be involved in the effort. Finally, students noted that parents and community members have been less involved in the planning process since the summer retreat, and they suggested that these people be brought back into the planning process. "At the last meetings, I was really disappointed. Parents and community members weren't there."

Theme four: Students believe that their voices are being heard, somewhat

Students in the focus groups began by stating that their voices were being heard. They felt that the principal was listening to them and even seeking out their opinions. As one student noted, "She comes to us with ideas and wants our help." But as they continued to speak, some of them began to modify or qualify what they were saying. As one student observed, the principal "has been listening. Teachers are starting to listen. Parents—I don't know. Parents are always the shaky ones."

Students stated that they enjoyed being involved in the planning meetings and other restructuring events. They believed that they have something important to say and claimed that they are willing to take responsibility to make changes happen. "They say they're treating us more like adults, but they're treating us more and more like juveniles." A few students felt that "even teachers" aren't really being listened to, unless what they say is in agreement with the direction that administration wants to take.

Again, however, students expressed an understanding of the difficulty of changing people's attitudes and beliefs about the role students should play. One student noted the difficulty in getting teachers to listen by suggesting, "I have trouble getting my parents to understand me!"

Theme five: Students have definite views about proposed changes

A move toward considering block scheduling seems to be the largest change being contemplated in the school. Attendance at workshops and site visits to schools that use block scheduling have been occurring throughout the fall semester. Students, teachers, parents, and community members have attended these sessions. The students voiced strong and varied opinions about the topic, and expressed the need for more information.

One student suggested that "if it's affecting us, [the principal] should go through us. We have ideas. I'm not a loose squirrel." Another student suggested there should be an assembly on the topic, with more than "just" adults talking about the new schedule. "Students from another school that has it [block scheduling] can come in and talk about it, answer questions. Students generally relate to other students better." A student who was strongly in favor of block scheduling noted that "if the only thing it does is get teachers to reevaluate how they teach, then it's good."

Discussion

From the above results we have drawn four tentative conclusions:

1. *Students have valuable ideas that they will voice if given the opportunity.* We were struck during the focus groups and during the Partnership meetings by the distinctive point of view of the students and the many useful and practical ideas they suggested. Many of their ideas are consistent with the ideas of the most acclaimed reformers. For example, a student's suggestion to implement one good idea instead of continually planning ideas is consistent with Fullan's (1991) suggestion to build on small successes during the initiation phase. Students, so often excluded from the change process, were also quick to note the absence of key stakeholders such as parents and community members, and they felt strongly that all groups needed to be represented. Finally, students offered a practical suggestion for communicating potential changes (like the move to block scheduling) to students through a school assembly.

There is evidence that students' voices are receiving serious consideration by other members of the school community. One student is chairing an action committee composed of students and teachers and has taken an active leadership role in restructuring efforts. Although Partnership activities are viewed as "just words" by some of the students who have been involved, there is an overwhelming sense that students appreciate having their ideas considered and believe that they have meaningful contributions to make to the restructuring efforts at their school.

2. *Including students in restructuring is consistent with constructivist learning objectives.* Student leaders are learning to work in groups, to communicate and collaborate with diverse groups of people, and they are learning about the change process. One student noted her views of the change process: "I don't think there is going to be, or needs to be, successes right now. It's my understanding that this is a planning year."

3. *Given the opportunity, students will try to make meaning out of proposed changes,* such as block scheduling. Fullan (1991) suggests that teachers need to make meaning out of proposed changes in order for those changes to be successful. In the focus groups, we saw students trying to do the same. Student leaders have started making meaning out of teachers' practices as they relate to the teaching and learning process. One student noted that "a lot of teachers have been teaching for a very long time. They use the same methods as when they began. It's harmful to students to have teachers teach in the same way." As Nieto (1994) found, through speaking out about their schooling experiences students began to think critically about their education and about the change processes at their schools.

4. *Involving students in restructuring may encourage greater student responsibility and caring about the school.* One student noted that in the past year "lots of activist groups have sprung up here. These groups actually care about the school. It's a lot more open here." Another student suggested that he was involved in the Partnership not for himself but for the students who would attend after he graduated: "I have one more year here. And hopefully during that

year we can do a lot more. But it's going to be the sophomores and freshmen who'll actually get to see it all working. And hopefully, they'll continue this."

Educational significance

Involving students in restructuring efforts in a meaningful fashion is rare. By highlighting this initiative, we hope to influence other educators to consider the benefit of including students when planning for educational change. Students, if given the opportunity, express strong and thoughtful opinions about their education. By providing a safe and systematic forum for them to do so, all stakeholders can gain new insights that might guide schools toward educational excellence. As evidenced by this study, students involved in the process may also benefit from their participation by improving their interpersonal skills and their understanding of organizational change.

In our other efforts to document restructuring at this urban high school we have been consistently impressed by student insights. The student leaders have participated wholeheartedly in planning meetings and have presented their beliefs clearly and oftentimes eloquently. Several times students have offered suggestions about process that have been embraced by other members of the Partnership, and they consistently offer meaningful contributions. One student leader summed up his beliefs about student voices in restructuring simply but confidently: "We have ideas."

References

Dunn, W., Basom, R. E. Jr., and Frantz, C. D. *Educational Policy Analysis: A Guide to Applications.* 1988.

Fullan, M. G., with Steigelbauer, S. *The New Meaning of Educational Change.* New York: Teachers College Press, 1991.

Fullan, M. G., and Miles, M. B. "Getting Reform Right: What Works and What Doesn't." *Phi Delta Kappan*, 1992, 73(10), 745–752.

Newmann, F. M., and Wehlage, G. *Successful School Restructuring.* Madison, Wis.: Center on Organization and Restructuring of Schools, 1995.

Nieto, S. "Lessons from Students on Creating a Chance to Dream." *Harvard Educational Review*, 1994, *64*(4), 392–426.

Villa, R. A., and Thousand, J. S. *Creating an Inclusive School*. Alexandria, Va.: Association for Supervision and Curriculum Development, 1995.

CYNTHIA J. REED *is a doctoral candidate at the School of Education, Program of Administrative Policy Studies, University of Pittsburgh.*

DAVID BECHTEL *is a research associate for the Mid-Atlantic Laboratory for School Success, Temple University.*

In Vermont's unique form of governor's school, high school students attend an intensive one-week summer institute on public issues and youth empowerment, then go on to take leadership and action in their schools and communities. The institute seeks to provide an atmosphere of intellectual challenge, emotional nurturance, and shared power, all key components in youth empowerment. Citing a supportive climate for sharing ideas, participants report increased confidence, skills, inspiration, and motivation. After attending the program, students have taken on community-service learning projects, initiated student activist groups, and presented the views of youth to adults at an educational conference and congressional hearing.

6

Empowering students to address current issues: The Vermont Governor's Institute on Public Issues and Youth Empowerment

John Ungerleider, Ange DiBenedetto

It was a powerful experience that showed me how one person can make a difference.
—High school student, Vermont Governor's Institute on Public Issues and Youth Empowerment

FOR THE PAST SEVEN SUMMERS, top students from high schools throughout Vermont have come together for an intensive, week-long institute on public issues, and have left describing ways in

NEW DIRECTIONS FOR SCHOOL LEADERSHIP, NO. 4, SUMMER 1997 © JOSSEY-BASS PUBLISHERS

which they have felt empowered to go on and take action in their schools and communities. The Vermont Governor's Institute on Public Issues and Youth Empowerment shares the goals of governor's schools nationally by providing enrichment for student excellence, yet it also provides a unique model as an adjunct to school-based programs. The institute's pedagogy is rooted in a model of youth empowerment that develops skills and confidence in a statewide core of student leaders in Vermont. Both as a program and as a pedagogical model, the institute recognizes the needs of motivated students to collaborate in an empowering context that could be more available or integrated as part of the secondary school curriculum.

There are governor's schools in twenty-five to thirty states around the country; the number fluctuates from year to year based on state funding. As determined by Tracy Cross's independent 1996 evaluation, the Governor's Institutes of Vermont (GIV) share many characteristics with governor's schools around the country, but they are structurally unique in terms of recruitment, funding, and length of programs. The selection of GIV participants is not based on their being tracked formally as gifted or talented students, which is the national norm for governor's schools; nevertheless, it is a rigorous process that identifies some of Vermont's promising students (Cross, 1996). Jean Olson, executive director of the GIV, describes a more flexible, more holistic approach used to identify motivated students—230 in all, from sixty-five schools. Students are recruited by the GIV through high school teachers and counseling offices for summer programs in the arts, sciences, and social studies. Olson points out that a small state like Vermont, with only sixty school districts, allows for personal contact between the GIV and the schools that may not be possible in other states. Vermont's institutes are designed to take representative students from every school district in the state, but participation has not been universal. According to Olson, the GIV is unique among the states as the only independent nonprofit organization running governor's schools. While the majority of governor's schools are totally state funded, the GIV is funded through a partnership: 20 percent state funding, 30 percent private donations, and 50 percent contributions from the individual public schools and from parents as tuition. Vermont is also unique in holding one- to two-week programs while the majority of governor's schools are three to six weeks long (J. Olson, interview with authors, November 1996).

Some governor's schools, notably those in New Jersey and Washington State, have attempted to influence the lives of students in ways that go beyond curricular knowledge by increasing students' social consciousness and capacity for action. In the Governor's Institute on Public Issues and Youth Empowerment, Vermont's social studies institute, faculty and students build a working environment of intellectual challenge, emotional nurturance, and shared power. These have been identified as key elements in the development of youth empowerment (DiBenedetto, 1991). This conceptual framework provides a lens through which to assess the impact on students of the Governor's Institute program, a model of an off-campus approach with potential for empowering students on campus.

The core curriculum of the public issues institute provides *intellectual challenges* to the students through simulations and presentations about contemporary issues, synthesized through small group discussion and journal writing. In classes held throughout the week, students focus on contemporary global and local issues. The faculty assists students in building a community of mutual respect and *emotional nurturance* in which conscious efforts are made to build inclusive friendships rather than to split into cliques. Faculty at the Institute *share power* with students, not by abdicating adult responsibility and decision making but by soliciting student input into the development of program policies and activities.

Although many youth-oriented programs provide intellectual challenges and others provide emotional support, how many truly share power with youth, or attempt to do all three in combination? Students at the Institute on Public Issues and Youth Empowerment evidence a personal sense of mutual empowerment that emerges during a challenging, supportive experience.

During the past two decades, the concept of power has been personalized as "empowerment" and has come to be seen as integral to effective cooperation instead of as domination. Surrey (1987,

p. 3) concludes that "personal empowerment can be viewed only through the larger lens of power through connection, i.e., through the establishment of mutually empathic and mutually empowering relationships." Kreisberg (1992) defines power in terms of "power with" rather than "power over."

Youth empowerment has been incorporated into youth programs using more or less comprehensive definitions of the concept. In the early 1980s, the National Commission on Resources for Youth published *Youth Empowerment: A Training Guide* (Whitham, 1982) and defined youth empowerment as "the process by which young people learn through active participation in the relationships, events, and institutions that affect their lives, to develop and apply their capacity to transform themselves and the world in which they live." Kielsmeier (1988) defines youth empowerment as young people perceiving themselves as powerful through "guided participation in acts of leadership, citizenship, and community service." Wasserman (1987) names respect as a key component of youth empowerment. Respect is defined as a combination of recognizing youth—who they are and what they do; nonjudgmentally accepting young people's thoughts and feelings; and valuing their decisions and life choices. With respect comes confidence, positive self-image, and a feeling of control over one's life. These are all essential aspects of empowerment.

The youth empowerment model presented in Figure 6.1 illustrates the three fundamental elements of the framework used by the Vermont institute to design and facilitate its program. The first element is *intellectual challenges*, which include (1) education and training, (2) the gaining of skills for critical analysis, and (3) the development of youths' ability and confidence to speak their minds and feel valued for their contributions to society. The second element, *emotional nurturance*, consists of (1) acceptance of diversity, (2) expression of opinions and emotions, and (3) creation of an environment of safety, closeness, and mutual appreciation. The third element is *shared power*, which consists of (1) adult leadership that is nonauthoritarian, exhibits unconditional acceptance, and

Figure 6.1. Youth empowerment model

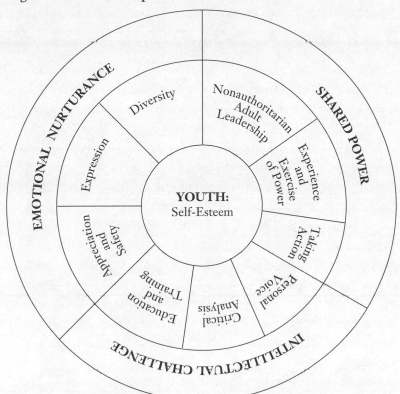

I. **Intellectual Challenge**
 A. Education and training
 B. Critical analysis
 C. Development of a personal
 voice

II. **Emotional Nurturance**
 A. Acceptance of diversity
 B. Expression of opinion and
 emotion; conflict resolution
 C. Safety, closeness, and
 appreciation

III. **Shared Power**
 A. Adult leadership
 1. Nonauthoritarian
 2. Unconditional
 acceptance
 3. Shared information and
 power
 B. Youth experience and
 exercise of power
 1. Individually
 2. Collectively
 C. Taking action

shares information and power; (2) youth individually and collectively experiencing and exercising power; and (3) youth taking
action for social change (DiBenedetto, 1992). These elements will
be discussed in more detail later in this chapter.

The participant data used in this chapter was collected through
(1) a written student evaluation of the 1996 institute administered
at the end of the week, (2) a survey of previous institute graduates,
(3) the final report of a follow-up community action project that
took place in the summer of 1996 under the auspices of a grant
from the Vermont State Commission on National and Community
Service, and (4) an independent evaluation of the GIV conducted
in 1996 by Tracy Cross of Ball State University, who allowed us to
access the data he gathered through student questionnaires. All
quotes are from students who have completed the institute.

Long-term impact on students: Individual cases

In assessing some of the long-term impacts on graduates of the
institute, it became clear that dormant leadership skills emerged in
students and were sustained within a group context of challenge,
stimulation, and support by peers and adults. The reflections of a
few graduates years later present an image of group energy and
enthusiasm, of participants meeting other students with similar
motivation, of recognition and encouragement by adult role models, and of a shared, mutually supportive experience that motivates
participants both within and beyond the program. Graduates report
how the inspiration and skills they developed at the institute have
assisted them in undertaking social action projects in their high
schools and communities.

One early graduate of the institute, "Kyle," who participated
when the institute was focused on international affairs, attributes
his enhanced empowerment to think and act critically and to take
political action to the supportive environment of the institute. Kyle
writes:

In high school I was inquisitive about public issues and student government and I was also shy, reserved and lacking in self confidence. . . . I certainly learned the information and rules about being a student and yet I do not recall having the ability to envision possibilities other than those demarcated for me by adults. A significant shift in my understanding of myself regarding learning occurred during the Governor's Institute. Facilitating a small group discussion and doing so competently, I felt a sense of confidence in which I felt the ability to ask questions and envision and articulate possible ways for understanding the topic at hand. I felt validated and confident in my own abilities to think and converse and likewise I felt a greater level of engagement and efficacy in the discussions.

Kyle cites how the level of expectations at the institute leads to students "rising to the occasion," and consequently to an increased enjoyment and satisfaction in the realization of their own abilities.

Another graduate of the early years of the institute, "Joan," has gone on to be a peace activist at her college, and she loves studying history. While the institute did not change her direction, it validated and energized her instincts. The key, to Joan, was in being around a large group of motivated students, as opposed to being in high school with a very small number of students motivated to make change in the world. In an institute workshop on student activism, Joan felt an "exciting, empowering solidarity in the room; students were energized by each other." This sharing was also multigenerational—in youth hearing adults' stories and older people hearing the students' stories, a synergy was created. The skills of leadership came from being in a room with other people who were there for the same reason. Yet for Joan the Governor's Institute was not primarily about gaining specific skills or knowledge but about the human exchange of energy, ideas, and inspiration.

For "Acadia," a more recent graduate of the Institute on Public Issues, discussions with other students at the institute helped her to clarify her beliefs as well as to get new skills and ideas about how to take leadership effectively: "It definitely made me feel clear about my beliefs. The simulation about power [Star Power] reaffirmed my belief in fighting for poor people even if I become rich." Acadia went on to start a student group working for the reelection of the local congressman, and she worked with the county campaign committee as well, liaisoning between the county organization and her school. "Talking with students from other schools gives you different ideas about what to do, about how to start a group." She is proud that her group "did more than any other student group has done." They have gone on since the election to create a progressive coalition that is developing a forum on child labor to educate students and community members about what actions can be taken in response to this issue.

Following the 1996 Governor's Institute, thirteen youth participants successfully initiated and maintained summer involvement in a variety of community-service learning projects concerned with public, social, and environmental issues around Vermont. Youth "returned to their towns and recognized they could find and fill an important niche in their own communities" (Habib and Reitz, 1996, p. 1). Students learned about the issues, about the role of government and individuals within their communities, and about the importance of skills and attitudes such as perseverance and confidence in addressing societal problems. They also saw the contribution that their initiative, involvement, and leadership in social action could make. One of the participants in this additional community-service segment of the institute connected principles she had considered at the institute with the actual experience of community service: "At the Governor's Institute, we discussed the idea that if everyone, or a significant number of people, would devote just a small amount of their time to better the community, then the world would be a better place for many. I now know this is true, for one person can indeed make a difference, no matter how small. My simple act of taking four or so hours from my week to work at an animal shelter has made the lives of others better."

Students reported feeling both valued and valuable in their communities, and that the community connections they made gave them support and motivation in carrying their summer service projects into the school year—including trying to establish community-service learning programs within their school's curriculum. One young man who participated in this community-service program writes: "Working at the recycling center has given me tremendous confidence in pursuing my original idea of making a community garden. I have made connections that would support me financially and people [who] would help me with the work. I have learned that you must advertise your idea heavily through pamphlets, newspapers, and local merchants. I have also learned that you should speak to every business, because the most unlikely people are likely to support you."

Three of the students who participated in the summer projects presented the results of their service work as part of a panel of rural, urban, and suburban youth at the Annual Regional Conference of the New England Environmental Educators Alliance in Lake Winnipesaukee, New Hampshire. They addressed a group of environmental educators interested in how best to serve the needs of youth.

The follow-up community-service work that this group of students did clearly developed their sense of themselves as social actors. They saw themselves empowered not only as student leaders but also as students who could be leaders in their communities—capable of assisting, influencing, and even leading adults in addressing important local problems with global ramifications.

Intellectual challenges

The explicit purpose of the Governor's Institute program, and one of the three elements in DiBenedetto's (1991) model, is intellectual challenge. Students are chosen for participation in the institute through an application process designed to bring in academically high-performing students as well as student leaders. The institute's curriculum is meant to simulate a week at college, with college faculty, challenging speakers, and intensive critical dialogue about complex issues. The curriculum is designed (1) to provide information and skill training, (2) to build students' ability to critically analyze issues, and (3) to help students develop a sense of personal voice.

Education and training

> *"The skills and knowledge I have gained here will carry me*
> *through my entire life."*

The core curriculum consists of focused issue groups led by faculty members on topics including politics, social justice, human ecology, community development, conflict resolution, and student activism. Each student chooses one group, in which he or she gets a mixture of lecture, experiential exercises, discussion, field trips, videos, and reading.

Training is not just informational; it is also experiential and develops skills. For example, the Star Power simulation mentioned earlier dynamically raises issues of inequality, challenging students to problem solve, recognize power dynamics, and directly wrestle with injustice and arbitrary authority.

Critical analysis

> *"To give us things to think about and then to have us*
> *solve them is very satisfying."*

Students are exposed to a broad range of opinions about stimulating and controversial topics. This sometimes includes contradictory information that stimulates critical analysis. A goal of the institute is to expand what is traditionally covered in public schools; in fact, students express that they are not exposed to this range of information as part of their regular high school curriculum.

Guest lecturers address a variety of global issues, followed by small-group discussion in which the students are encouraged to think critically about the often powerful visions or controversial positions of the speakers. In addition to Vermont's Senator Patrick Leahy and Congressman Bernard Sanders, as well as various state senators and representatives from Vermont, speakers have included Vietnam veteran and activist Brian Wilson, South Vietnamese refugee author Jade Ngoc Huynh, civil rights activists Wally and

Juanita Nelson, and Navajo educator Ferlin Clark. The founders of the Center for Living Democracy, Frances Moore Lappé and Paul Du Bois, addressed participatory democracy in America; members of the Gay/Lesbian Youth Speaker's Bureau recounted their experiences with stereotypes and homophobia; ex-gang members described their experiences of gang life; and University of Vermont environmental studies professor William Eddy presented a vision of our species' place in the universe.

Development of a personal voice

> *"Just being more educated on specific issues will now allow me to speak my mind because I know what I am talking about."*

The institute offers a range of activities that facilitate student self-expression. Learning how to develop a voice for their perspective is critical to these young people. One of the most moving moments for us as directors is when we hear students reveal how they have found their voices. Articulating and expressing their beliefs is an empowering process for youth. The result of having such a voice is that teens feel they can take action and make a difference in society. As one participant noted, "Attending the Institute on Public Issues motivated me to be more vocal in my student government and community activities because it allowed me to see my ideas and their potential."

Student evaluations showed that the students responded most to the activities that touched them in personal ways: "I did not only learn about the issues, I learned how to deal with them on a very personal level." Students reported how important it was to speak up and be listened to in order to believe in themselves and feel acknowledged as important contributing members of the institute. Students even expressed that they felt all right about being "smart," whereas in school they often believed they must "dumb down" to be accepted. As participants learned to speak out, they developed a sense of pride, power, and purpose.

Emotional nurturance

The second element of the youth empowerment model, emotional nurturance, consists of providing an atmosphere that (1) accepts diversity, (2) allows expression of opinions and emotions, and (3) provides an opportunity for participants to feel safety, closeness, and appreciation for one another. An atmosphere of interpersonal support provides a sense of emotional safety for self-expression at the Governor's Institute. Feeling accepted and appreciated by peers and staff provides a context for young people to feel unafraid to share thoughts and feelings.

Acceptance of diversity

"This is a place where you feel accepted."

All institute participants are accepted and valued, regardless of their personal history, in a supportive, collegial community. Cliques often form, but within the context of the larger group a process is facilitated by staff in which the exclusionary barriers can be broken down and broader friendships may develop. A midweek community meeting allows students to work through potential problems and reach a higher level of group functioning and mutual respect. As a result of naming the group dynamics and issues that emerge by mid-week, students typically bond into a tight-knit group, surprised and impressed at their ability to overcome the teenage tendency to break into small cliques.

Expression of opinions and emotions

"I feel empowered because I feel like people listen to my ideas."

The week is structured to let students express their opinions after guest presentations and in small focus groups. Students need to be heard, to get airtime, to acknowledge that both their opinions and feelings matter. An atmosphere is created that demonstrates that faculty really want to know what students are thinking, feeling, and struggling to understand. Students report that they feel safe to express their opinions and to engage in dialogue with peers as well as with adults. The safety to express dissenting and diverse opinions and not be personally criticized leads to mutual and self-respect. As one student noted, "I had an opinion and no one else could understand it because it was a touchy subject that a lot of times is a battle of the sexes. I felt like it was me against thirty other students! But I stood my ground and now I'm respected!"

Students carry the confidence to express their own viewpoint beyond the week-long institute: "I will be more brave and comfortable about speaking up about issues I think are important."

Safety, Closeness, and Appreciation

"I liked how everybody cared and they weren't afraid to show it."

Student enthusiasm for the week is significantly due to the people students meet and the friendships they form. In program evaluations, students have described how they "got so close to people" and experienced "a week of bonding as a family." One participant wrote: "I made friends and contacts that I foresee lasting for the rest of my life."

The institute first came to the School for International Training, a college located in Brattleboro, Vermont, in 1989. It was known then as the Governor's Institute on International Affairs. Sixty high school students, including sixteen visiting students from Russia, were housed throughout the university campus as roommates of the international students. Although this approach exposed the institute participants to important diversity, the group size is now limited to forty participants so they can live together in one dormitory, which allows them to get to know each other fairly well during the short time they are together. Junior faculty live in the dormitory with the students and are critical role models in the team-building process.

Recreation activities assist in building community. These include basketball and soccer games, videos, sing-alongs, and a field trip for swimming and strawberry picking. To celebrate the community that has developed during the week, the last night of the institute is a dance; an evening of rock and roll, contra, or klezmer dancing is followed by a bonfire with "s'mores" and singing.

It is not just an atmosphere of safety and intimacy that builds a cohesive community; it is also the mutual respect and appreciation that grows out of struggling together with issues of common concern: "I'm going away from this institute with a greater appreciation and understanding that you really have to listen, care for, and respect people." The faculty try to model the respect, acceptance, and care that help the students feel safe with and close to one another.

Shared power

The third element of the youth empowerment model used at the Governor's Institute is giving youth the opportunity to share power with faculty, to take leadership in the institute. The week includes many ways of teaching about power and power dynamics. The Star Power simulation raises the issues of economic inequality and fairness. The goal of the simulation is to challenge students to create strategies for overcoming injustice. It also provides an opportunity for students to discuss their perceptions of youth disempowerment in our society, and it serves as a model for reflection all week long when issues of power and leadership arise. Students are able to connect this experiential learning to their own experiences of disempowerment as youth and to take back a sense of power. As one student noted, "The activities like Star Power and others put me in a position of leadership."

Sharing power with youth requires (1) adult leadership that is nonauthoritarian, gives unconditional acceptance to youth, and shares information as well as decision-making power; (2) giving youth experience in exercising power—both individually and collectively; and (3) giving youth opportunities to take action.

Adult leadership

"I found adults who don't think of us as just kids and it was very inspiring."

A key to student perception of shared power is whether the adult is speaking from his or her own experience, from his or her heart, and not talking down to the students. Students feel that adult leaders express genuine respect for them by listening to them and including them in decision making: "I feel empowered because the people here talk with us rather than to us or at us." For example, participants expressed dissatisfaction about a mandatory lights-out time. This led to student-adult dialogue in which a process of respectful negotiation emerged, taking into account all needs, along with the question of rights versus responsibilities. In successfully resolving the issue, students felt heard and respected as young adults. In addition, they accepted their responsibility to one another and to the teaching goals of the faculty. A potential power struggle between adults and young people became a win-win situation. Students reported that such respect was not given in other student government programs they had attended in the past.

Youth experience and exercise of power

"The institute gave me self-confidence to succeed in a leadership role. Others at the institute were leaders, which inspired me to be also. . . . Being with other kids who feel empowered made me feel like I can succeed also."

The process of petitioning to eliminate a lights-out time and negotiating with faculty for the freedom to prove students could share responsibility for the institute's schedule led to a direct sense of youth empowerment. According to students, "the curfew experience was empowering; we had a sense of responsibility. We had to self-police ourselves and the process was a good learning experience." "We obviously have been empowered through being able to propose a later bedtime. I feel we have the opportunity to change most of the things in this institute."

Students also have input in developing program content. While at the institute, students lead workshops. Topics have included the Holocaust and anti-Semitism, reproductive rights, and international freedom songs. Students do final presentations about the meaning of youth empowerment in terms of the issues they focus on during the week. For example, students focusing on human ecology have designed and developed a pamphlet on strategies for environmental action to be distributed in Vermont high schools, and participants focusing on student activism did guerrilla theater in the cafeteria about AIDS awareness. Even within the limited parameters of the institute, the experience of themselves as informed activists proved empowering to students: "Now I know that you can at least try to change things that you don't agree with and I know the ways to go about it."

One year, students made presentations on youth issues to Congressman Bernie Sanders, who responded specifically to their ideas. The opportunity for meaningful dialogue with national leaders such as Congressman Sanders and Senator Leahy has made students feel respected as potential future leaders. Students have also written various policy proposals to Vermont governor Howard Dean.

Proposing changes in state and national policy, educating one another, and collaboratively taking steps to educate their peers around the state have given participants a tangible experience of their ability to effect change: "It made me see that I as a teenager have power to do things that affect the world I live in." A sense of personal and collective power is a critical factor in the development of student potential for empowerment.

Taking action

*"I felt as though I could accomplish any task before me and I did.
I started a utensil recycling program at my school and changed
our senior class council's unfair decisions."*

The experience of youth empowerment has not been limited to on-campus simulations of activism. Community-service learning is integrated into the program and is used as a follow-up to the week by interested students who want an experience of taking action in response to a local issue. During the week of the institute, students spend half of one day participating in community service with several local organizations—an environmental education center, a senior center, community supported agriculture, and an AIDS education project. After the institute, opportunities for participation in community-service learning projects in students' home communities has been supported under the auspices of a grant from the Vermont State Commission on National and Community Service. In 1996, half of the institute graduates committed themselves to participating in this additional community-service program. Participants received ongoing faculty support during a focused six-week session and certificates for their community service. Youth carried on a dialogue, with each other as well as with faculty, about the learning that took place for them by doing community work. Three students presented their work at an adult conference on social action.

Graduates of previous institutes have gone on to do their own activism and community service. According to one student, "as soon as the institute was over I started new community projects and fought for student rights at school." Graduates of the 1995 institute made a presentation at a congressional hearing on youth issues in Burlington, Vermont, organized by Congressman Sanders.

Conclusion

Students in the Vermont Governor's Institute on Public Issues and Youth Empowerment felt that their horizons were broadened not only through obtaining new information about public issues but also by gaining a sense of personal empowerment—a feeling that they could make a difference or assume leadership. Our overriding sense in reviewing the impact of the institute was that it empowered students to become more fully who they are. It did not so much transform them as it facilitated a blossoming of the potentials in an already capable group of students.

For the adults running this institute, the youth empowerment model is a useful framework for designing and facilitating the program as well as for responding to students' needs throughout the week. It is very easy for adults not to want to share power or decision making with youth. It feels risky to let inexperienced youth share in key responsibilities. The fact that they are legally minors and must follow certain restrictions on behavior is unavoidable. The result of a balanced response to youth demands, however, has proven to be rewarding. The key words are *shared power*. Adults can be guides in a manner that consults youth and seeks to respect mutual needs—including the one for adults to retain the authority necessitated by legal responsibility. How much power can be shared with students on campus is a question that could lead to an exciting, empowering dialogue with youth.

High-achieving students who are socially conscious and active can feel isolated and discouraged in their high schools, as students report when they arrive at the summer institute. Finding peer support from like-minded students from around the state has been significant for students, who return to school energized and motivated to take leadership on current issues. The brief immersion in a stimulating program like the Governor's Institute on Public Issues and Youth Empowerment can provide students with a critical boost to their emerging self-image as capable agents of social change. Could students be getting such support and encouragement in their schools as well?

Teachers can use the youth empowerment model to support students who seek to integrate into their high schools the competencies they gained over the summer, at a governor's school or elsewhere. Teachers and administrators can be conscious of sharing power in decision making on campus, upholding a level of intellectual challenge for top students, and creating an atmosphere of emotional nurturance for young people who are challenging themselves to maturely address the problems of our time.

An independent governor's institute like Vermont's can be seen as an important adjunct to gifted secondary education in social studies—an adjunct that might be expanded to involve more students, particularly those motivated student leaders who excel in certain areas and care about social issues yet are not tracked as gifted. Within Vermont, social studies teachers and guidance counselors could be more involved in nominating competent students who are likely to thrive in the Governor's Institutes.

As youth take on responsibility and grow in confidence and self-esteem, they feel powerful and capable of effecting change in their own lives as well as in their communities and schools. One student reflected, "I left with exactly the knowledge I needed to make myself a better person in this world." A short, intensive program that attends directly to the needs of youth to be recognized, respected, and challenged to improve their world evidently facilitates a surge of empowerment that students take back to their schools and communities as incipient leaders and activists.

References

Cross, T. *Evaluation of 1996 Governor's Institutes of Vermont.* Muncie, Ind.: Ball State University, 1996.

DiBenedetto, A. "An Analysis of Youth Empowerment Through Group Involvement." Unpublished doctoral dissertation, Department of Education, University of Massachusetts at Amherst, 1991.

DiBenedetto, A. "Youth Groups: A Model for Empowerment." *Networking Bulletin: Empowerment and Family Support,* 1992, *2*(3), 19–24.

Habib, D., and Reitz, E. "Building a Statewide Community Service Learning Network: The Governor's Institute on Public Issues and Youth Empowerment." Final Grant Report to the Vermont State Commission on National and Community Service, 1996.

Kielsmeier, J. *Outdoor Centers and Camps: A "Natural" Location for Youth Leadership Development.* New Mexico: Eric Cress, 1988.

Kreisberg, S. *Transforming Power: Domination, Empowerment and Education.* New York: State University of New York Press, 1992.

Surrey, J. *Relationship and Empowerment.* Wellesley, Mass.: Wellesley College, 1987.

Wasserman, S. "Enabling Children to Develop Personal Power Through Building Self-Respect." *Childhood Education,* 1987, *32*(4), 293–294.

Whitham, M. *Youth Empowerment: A Training Guide.* Boston: National Commission of Resources for Youth, 1982.

Additional Resources

Gordon, S. "Encouraging Student Leadership." *International School Journal,* 1994, *14*(1), 43–51.

Jackins, H. *Young and Power Journal.* Seattle: Rational Island, 1988.

Langstaff, D. *Teens as Community Resources: A Model of Youth Empowerment.* New York: Plan for Social Excellence, 1991.

JOHN UNGERLEIDER is associate professor of peace and conflict studies in the bachelor's program in world issues at the School for International Training in Brattleboro, Vermont, and director of the Vermont Governor's Institute on Public Issues and Youth Empowerment.

ANGE DIBENEDETTO is a therapist and educational consultant, an adjunct faculty at the School for International Training in Brattleboro, Vermont, and assistant director of the Vermont Governor's Institute on Public Issues and Youth Empowerment.

As peer mediation programs become increasingly popular and effective methods for stemming violence and changing the climate of schools, some researchers and practitioners look for additional program benefits to schools and students. The preliminary study presented in this chapter explored the possible link between the skills of student mediators and leadership development. Twenty-nine student mediators from three urban high schools in eastern Massachusetts participated in a survey and focus group sessions to begin the process of defining leadership in a high school setting. As the participants identified the elements that enable mediators to mediate conflict successfully among their peers, several themes emerged that pointed to elements of personal growth and development that enabled them to function also as leaders.

7

Understanding student leadership through peer mediation

Patricia Ensell Trela, Michael J. Conley

THE PURPOSE OF THE PRELIMINARY STUDY presented in this chapter was to explore whether the skills and sensitivities demonstrated by student mediators as a result of mediator training and their experiences as "helpers" during the peer mediation process can be linked to leadership development. The study was designed to begin the process of defining what student leadership is in a school setting, and to identify some of the skills demonstrating leadership that mediators feel they have used during mediation and that have

NEW DIRECTIONS FOR SCHOOL LEADERSHIP, NO. 4, SUMMER 1997 © JOSSEY-BASS PUBLISHERS

transferred to various situations in school, at home, and in their community.

Peer mediation has become an increasingly popular and effective method for stemming violence in schools and for teaching conflict resolution skills to students. One of the reasons for the popularity of peer mediation in middle and high schools is that peer mediation provides a nonthreatening environment in which students involved in conflict situations may begin to explore their feelings and to understand another person's situation or their motives for behavior (Allen, 1993). The mediation process assists students with the development of creative solutions to conflict situations and attempts to preserve their relationships through a review of their behaviors, the consequences, and the alternatives.

Research on the success of peer mediation as a conflict resolution strategy has focused on the changes that take place during mediation for the individual parties involved in a conflict situation (Bush and Folger, 1994; Bush, 1995), and on how changes in attitudes and behaviors affect the climate of the school (Cutrona and Guerin, 1994). Measures of the success of a specific peer mediation program have been quantified as the number of agreements upheld after mediation and the reduction in the number of suspensions, detentions, and violent incidents reported by schools (Cutrona and Guerin, 1994; Prothrow-Stith, 1991).

For some researchers and practitioners in the field of conflict resolution and violence prevention in schools, these measures do not fully represent the contribution of mediation programs to changing the behaviors and attitudes of the students involved in mediation programs as mediators, nor do they begin to address the life skills that are developed by the mediators, or the changes in the climate of schools as a result of the positive role modeling and leadership of student mediators. According to Bush (1995), the moral and leadership development potential of the mediation process can be measured by looking at the growth of mediators trained in specific approaches to mediation, specifically transformative mediation, and evaluating the experiences that promote growth and develop skills in students as they participate in these programs. In reviewing the limited research on the effectiveness of peer mediation training for the mediators, Johnson and Johnson (1995) found that a few studies indicated that when students were trained, and successfully learned conflict resolution procedures and strategies, and had an opportunity to practice their skills, they could apply their skills not only in school settings but also in situations outside the school.

Cutrona and Guerin (1994) reviewed the benefits of peer mediation for the mediators and found that mediators enhanced their language and communication skills, increased their self-esteem, learned problem-solving techniques, increased their status, and influenced their peers. At the bottom of the list of benefits was that mediators develop leadership as a result of training and participation in the mediation program. These results do not, however, explain what leadership is for mediators in a school setting.

Mediators receive extensive training in how to conduct the mediation process for the parties involved. They develop their communication and listening skills in order to understand interpersonal relationships and become aware of the differences among people and their styles of coping with conflict situations. Even though many of these competencies can be said to be true of leaders, mediators regard themselves as helpers of their peers rather than as leaders in their schools. It is during the mediation training that mediators learn how to "help" the parties in conflict communicate their positions, listen to each other's viewpoints, clarify any misunderstandings, identify the issues, and reach a resolution. As a result of the skills demonstrated by the mediators, the parties often develop a recognition of their power to make positive choices when faced with conflict situations.

The question asked by the current research was: As mediators develop stronger interpersonal skills themselves, form trusting relationships with their peers and adults, and advocate nonviolent resolution to conflict as a result of being trained as a mediator and participating in the peer mediation program, are they moving beyond the role of mediator into the role of leader?

What is leadership?

Woyach (1992) cites Bennis and Nanus's observation that "leadership is one of the most studied but least understood of all social phenomena" (p. 2). Researchers and practitioners have studied leadership by looking at the elements of leadership, such as traits, personality characteristics, "born or made" greatness, group facilitation, goal attainment, effectiveness, goodness, style—and the list goes on and on (Rost, 1991, p.7). Rost's contribution to the study of leadership is a view of leadership as relational, "the connection that developed among leaders and followers" (p. 8), and not just something leaders do for their followers. He feels that all that is needed is a list of elements or priorities that researchers, scholars, and practitioners can use to measure and try to understand how leadership works.

Even though many questions about leadership development are still unanswered, "over half a million high school students, along with a growing number of middle school students, participate in programs intended to encourage civic leadership and to develop leadership skills" (Woyach, 1992, p.2). However, the ongoing debates over the best methods to use for leadership development are bringing researchers closer to an agreement on some of the essential elements of leadership. Woyach defined leadership development as containing elements that are "essential for individuals to organize themselves, establish goals and priorities, make decisions, settle conflicts and accomplish their goals" (p. 3).

Methods and materials

The participants involved in this preliminary study were twenty-nine student mediators, nine male and twenty female, from three urban high school mediation programs in eastern Massachusetts. The mediators were an ethnically and economically diverse group that mirrored, as closely as possible, the diversity of their schools. The mediators ranged in age from fifteen to twenty-two years old and represented grades 10, 11, and 12. All of the mediators were trained using the Student Conflict Resolution Experts (S.C.O.R.E.) model of mediation training and program development provided by the Office of the Attorney General (OAG) for the Commonwealth of Massachusetts (see Exhibit 7.1). The level of experience as a S.C.O.R.E. mediator ranged from no mediations to twenty mediations.

Exhibit 7.1. Summary of Student Conflict Resolution Experts (S.C.O.R.E.) document prepared by Mediation Services, Massachusetts Attorney General's Office

Massachusetts Attorney General Scott Harshbarger has set as one of the priorities of his office the reduction of urban violence in all its various forms. One of the most critical problems facing society today is the level of violence in its schools. S.C.O.R.E. is a program created by the Office of the Attorney General (OAG) that seeks to reduce violent conflict in urban schools and to bring hope for a brighter future to young people. S.C.O.R.E. provides grants for the development of school-based mediation programs using trained student mediators to resolve violent and potentially violent conflict among their peers.

The model for S.C.O.R.E. is unique. The OAG gives S.C.O.R.E. grants to community mediation programs and requires that matching funds be raised. Funds are used to hire a full-time coordinator, who works in the targeted school to develop and run the mediation program. The coordinator's responsibilities include outreach and referrals, recruiting and training mediators, scheduling and supervising the mediation sessions, and following up on agreements. Typically, mediations involve fights, threats, harassment, and rumors among students who know one another. The OAG collects data from all programs and provides training and technical assistance as needed.

Student mediators are chosen because they have shown enthusiasm for resolving conflicts in a nonviolent way. An effort is made to recruit a group of students that represents a true cross section of the student body. The training for the students and teachers is conducted by experienced trainers from the OAG and community mediation programs. The twenty-to twenty-five-hour training program involves role-plays, skill-building exercises, and games that are designed to provide an enjoyable and intense learning experience. Through the training, students learn the value of listening, using neutral language, not taking sides, and looking beneath the surface for the real cause of the conflict.

The methods of inquiry included a brief survey and focus group sessions. The survey was designed to assess mediators' perceptions of their role in the classroom, schoolwide, and with peers in general, and to assess how those roles might have changed as a result of being trained as a mediator, participating in a peer mediation program, and participating in the mediation process.

Mediators responded to a series of statements on a survey about how they felt their peers, teachers, and school administrators perceived them as a result of their mediation training and participation in the mediation process. Other statements on the survey dealt with specific experiences related to being a mediator and with the mediators' perceived self-confidence in their skills to handle these situations.

For each statement response, the choice ranged from 1, which indicated that the mediator strongly disagreed with the statement, to 5, which indicated that the mediator strongly agreed with the statement. A 3 represented a neutral response to the statement or served as a midpoint between strongly disagree and strongly agree. At the end of the survey, an open-ended question asked the mediators to identify the "one best thing about being a mediator." The open-ended format of this question provided some insight into individual benefits of peer mediation training and program involvement that could be linked to leadership. The survey also acted as a prompt to the focus groups that followed it.

The focus group method was selected for two reasons. First, because there has been a lack of research in the area of peer mediation as a promoter of student leadership, focus groups can provide a rich data source as well as multiple lines of inquiry for future research (Krueger, 1988; Patton, 1987). Second, focus groups might offer insight into the reasons that students adopt leadership roles, and they might begin to define what leadership is in a school setting.

The focus groups were small—two groups of ten participants and one group of nine participants. One session was conducted for each school and each session lasted approximately seventy-five minutes. Focus group members were asked to comment on whether peer mediation had affected their social relationships with peers, teachers, and administrators; on their career goals; and on their academic interests. Each focus group session concentrated on the mediators' willingness to identify with problem solvers, especially identified leaders in the school, as well on as their ability to deal effectively with conflict in different situations. The sessions were tape-recorded. Transcripts of the focus groups were prepared from the tapes and analyzed to identify common themes among participants.

Survey results and discussion

The results of the survey indicate that 60 percent of the mediators participating in the study became mediators as a result of being successfully mediated. The mediation process was such a positive and successful experience for them that they were encouraged to become mediators so they could help other people who were struggling with conflict in their lives.

The mediators reported high levels of agreement (more than 3.50) with statements that they related to their peers differently (M = 4, SD = .95), listened to both sides of a story (M = 4.43, SD = .61), changed the way they dealt with personal conflict (M = 4.42, SD = .68), thought more independently (M = 3.64, SD = 1.18), and surprised people with their mediation skills (M = 4.15, SD = .71) as a result of mediation training and participating in the mediation process. The mediators reported low levels of agreement (less than 3.50) with statements regarding how their peers (M = 3.41, SD = .87), teachers (M = 3.21, SD = .80), or school administrators (M = 3.33, SD = .84) perceive them since they became trained as mediators; but in the focus group sessions, mediators talked about specific situations in which their peers, teachers, and school administrators expressed their admiration for the work of mediators. The mediators felt that they were often treated with more respect by most people in their schools who knew what they did (as mediators) for their school, and therefore they worked hard to live up to that level of respect.

Mediators were asked to identify the "one best thing about being a mediator." The responses ranged from "acquiring new skills," "learning how to listening for information and communicate better," and "meeting different people," by mediators with limited mediation experience, to "makes you feel like a role model for the school," "learned how to value the opinion of others more," "developing more patience," and "being trusted to help people with their problems and they respect you for it," by mediators with more mediation experience. The responses of the mediators with limited mediation experience focused on the skills of interpersonal relationships and the excitement of "meeting different people," such as mediators from other schools, school administrators, college faculty, professionals, and politicians, as well as other students involved in mediation as parties. Responses from the mediators with more mediation experience focused less on the skills developed as a result of being trained to mediate and the participation in the mediation program and more on the behaviors, feelings, and attitudes that strengthened their relationships with other people.

These student mediators felt that becoming a more patient person and being trusted and respected by others were important qualities that were developing as a result of participating in the mediation program and involved more than using the skills learned in mediation training. Rost (1991) defined leadership as "a process whereby leaders and followers relate to one another to achieve a purpose" (p. 8). These qualities may provide us with an understanding of leadership as relational. During the mediation, mediators and the parties relate to one another in order to achieve a resolution to a conflict situation. After the mediation, mediators feel that some of their peers related to them as leaders, as people trusted with confidential information and respected and admired for their skill level and dedication to conflict resolution. It appears from the survey results that the more mediators mediate, the higher the level of confidence they have in the use of their skills and the more they value an open, trusting, and respectful relationship with their peers.

Focus group results and discussion

Several themes emerged from the focus group sessions: neutrality, self-control, personal efficacy, changes in others' perceptions of the mediators, and improvement of the mediators' emotional states. Mediators identified some important changes in communicating with and relating to their peers and to the adults in school and at home as a result of participating in the program. They clearly felt that the peer mediation program had helped them to communicate with more assurance and sensitivity; to relate to adults, even adults in authority, in a positive way; and to behave as persons of responsibility and integrity. They also felt that they were more willing to deviate from what they perceived to be the expectations of their peers. All of these improvements in their interpersonal skills point to experiences in leadership development that the mediators participating in this study considered important and valuable for all students in school.

Neutrality

One of the most common themes to emerge from the focus group discussions was the ability to "stay neutral," "be objective," or "remain nonjudgmental." Each group mentioned that peer mediation had helped them to "listen to both sides of the story" without indicating to others involved in the mediation which party they might personally favor. The issue of staying neutral dovetails somewhat with other qualities described by mediators, such as improved communication skills, especially the primary communication skill of listening. What made staying neutral a valuable and distinct ability in the minds of the mediators was not only its obvious effect on communication in the mediation session, but also the inherent value of not jumping to conclusions and of keeping an open mind. One participant described this ability as possessing "discipline." The choice of the word *discipline* is noteworthy because it connotes that the ability to restrain oneself or focus oneself has value in and of itself. The degree to which neutrality was considered a significant accomplishment was impressive: twelve mediators volunteered without prompting that being able to remain "neutral," "open-minded," or "unbiased" was an important and valuable outcome of their experiences as mediators.

Self-control

Another common theme, closely related to the theme of neutrality, was self-control. Almost every student described himself or herself as more patient and less likely to act in anger than he or she used to be. For example, one student stated, "When I get into a fight with my friends, I used to want to explode but now I think to myself, 'Stop.' I just think, 'Stop'. . . just try to work it out with them." This self-control carried over to family conflicts. Family was one of the primary areas that mediators cited when asked where in their lives their peer mediation experience had made the greatest impact.

Neutrality and the ability to control impulses were clearly related to mediators' sense of their own efficacy. One mediator said: "Once you learn how to mediate, you learn how to get along. When you hear a problem, you don't just jump in with 'blah, blah, blah.' You are the big person about it and let them scream at you and you just say, 'I'm trying to talk with you civilized-like, why are you screaming at me?'" This ability to control herself has enabled this mediator to respond in a way in which she feels she is more likely to "get along" with a less mature but nevertheless important peer.

Personal efficacy

The broadest theme in the focus groups was becoming a more effective person. Comments that referred to the mediators' ability to act responsibly or with greater integrity, to be less shy or more willing to get involved, to act on a vision of the future with regard to personal goals, to be better able to communicate effectively, and to be able to make a positive impact on people in need were related to an increased sense of efficacy. Woyach (1992, p. 3) calls this efficacy the ability to "establish goals," "make decisions," and "accomplish goals." Mediators are clearly aware of the success of their work and show awareness of their increased confidence as a result of their success.

Responsibility. One aspect of efficacy the focus group participants discussed was responsibility. The peer mediators expressed an understanding of what it means to be responsible for their own lives. This came through most clearly when the mediators began discussing what it was like to have one of their own conflicts mediated: "You can't say to do one thing and don't do it yourself. . . . I think you have to be committed . . . and when you're a mediator you commit to [having your own conflicts mediated]."

Each of the members of this focus group agreed that having their own conflicts mediated was uncomfortable when strong feelings were involved but usually resulted in a positive experience. They agreed that it was very important to the integrity of the peer mediation program that all mediators take responsibility for their own conflicts and advocate nonviolence in the school, and that becoming peer mediators had made them more responsible persons in both areas.

The mediators who insisted that they themselves must follow the guidelines for mediation did not feel that they were involved in fewer conflicts: "If everybody in the building was a mediator, there wouldn't be less fights, but then again, people could settle their own fights." This opinion appears to argue that mediators are better able to take responsibility for their actions, although the actions themselves are not likely to change.

School involvement. Another way in which mediators showed a higher degree of efficacy since their exposure to the peer mediation program was in their increased willingness to become involved in school events and organizations. This increased involvement sometimes extended to accepting leadership roles in school organizations. One student stated that he felt that being a peer mediator established him as a leader in the minds of his peers. Another student described her experiences as starting off "not being involved in anything and now I'm involved with everything. It [peer mediation] started to bring me closer to the school. . . . I wasn't involved in a lot of school projects [but] you meet nice people like [the peer mediation staff and other mediators] and you get involved in student government. . . . [Now] I am the chairperson of the School Advisory Board." Another student said she had "never been involved" in her school before and because of her involvement with peer mediation she now feels she can help her friends and peers solve their problems instead of "just letting them do it."

Career goals. A third way in which the mediators demonstrated greater efficacy is in their awareness and interest in career and future goals. Six mediators shared their sense that the mediation experience had influenced their career choice: "I wanted to do something in business management, but when I came to mediation, I changed my mind and now I want to do communication with juveniles to help others. . . . I was like, wow! I should really try to help others." There were several references to mediation providing mediators with the skills necessary to succeed in any career path; for example: "I think the purpose of mediation is to solve conflict and wherever you go there will be conflict so regardless if you're going to work at McDonald's the rest of your life or be hired as a president, it will help you."

Communication. A fourth way in which mediators demonstrated greater efficacy was their almost unanimous sense of improved communication skills. Analysis of the mediators' comments suggests that the improvements in communication were due partially to a greater ability to hypothesize what others might be experiencing and partially to a greater confidence in their own ability to speak.

One mediator explained his increased ability to hypothesize in terms of his awareness of the potentials for misunderstanding: "You have to be very cautious of how you say things because people could get the wrong impression. That goes with every situation in life. You may want . . . to compliment a group of your friends every day on something. . . . Someone may hear that same compliment and misinterpret it."

The other component of improved communication skills is a sense of confidence, possibly coming from practice and training sessions but also perhaps stemming from the feeling that one has in the past and can again in the present make a difference. Students reported in each of the groups a newfound sense that their efforts were significant and that they could in fact make a difference in the situations in which they find themselves involved. This in turn creates a greater desire within the mediators to communicate effectively: "They [peer mediation coordinators] always called me for mediations so I felt good that I was helping someone and I learned a lot about how people interact and how you should interact with people."

Mediators noted also that their sense of self-efficacy was sufficient in that they were willing to take on even larger problems, often involving adults: "I do mediations because I find it interesting. . . . I'll give you an example [from home], when your parents fight over things that make little sense. . . . It's funny because I use the same process that I use here [in mediation]. They're angry and they don't want to listen to me so I just talk to them individually, and then together and oftentimes they end up kissing each other."

Others' perceptions

Another broad theme that the mediators discussed in the focus groups was changes they noted in others' perceptions of them, including changes in both their peers and adults.

Perceptions of peers. The changes in mediators' relationships to their peers seemed to have far more significance for the mediators than did the changes in the adults' perceptions. Many students noted that they were much more willing to deviate from what they perceived to be the expectations of their peers since becoming peer mediators. For instance, "now that I am more involved in mediation and my whole attitude has changed, whatever we are talking about or whatever we are saying, if there is a problem going on I don't say shut up. I try another way around it, I want to talk about it. It's not that I don't care, I just want you to know how I feel and what I think of you. At first, they were just like shocked, because I wasn't like that before, but now they are getting used to it, because I've been mediating for a while."

Shock is not an uncommon description of peers' responses to the mediators' attitudes. Disappointment, or at least a sense of loss, was also prevalent: "Before I did mediation, anytime there'd be a conflict I'd be right there with my friends. Every time there's a conflict now, my friends are like, 'Oh, we can't ask him anymore. He's the one who solves everything.'"

Not all peers viewed the changes as negative. Another mediator described her friends as not seeing all of the changes she herself had undergone: "I see it more myself than they see it, but they see it and now they call me the mediator. Not because I'm in this program, but just because of what I do. I listen to their problems and I give them good advice . . . but I can also be neutral. . . . That comes through training."

Many of the mediators related instances in which their peer mediation responsibilities overrode the social expectations of their friends and other important peers. For instance: "I did a mediation before with my best friend and a person who I cannot stand and naturally my friend wanted me to take her side, but I just said, 'Hey, you know the process, you've been here ten times.'" The responsibility extends even beyond immediate peers into social groups and powerful cultural forces. One mediator who identified herself as Spanish said, "If I'm doing a mediation with a Spanish kid and she wants me to be on [her] side . . . I must keep reminding her that I'm neutral."

Perceptions of adults. The groups were almost unanimous in noting the way they as mediators had changed in the perceptions of their peers, but they were much less unanimous regarding the perceptions of adults. Several students responded that they felt being a mediator had improved the perceptions that adults, usually teachers, had of them. For example: "A lot of my teachers know me and know what I do [mediate] and I have had teachers come to me with problems with other students in class . . . and use me to listen to [the students]." The mediator clearly felt that the teacher values the mediator's skills and considers her a leader. This student had previously felt that teachers in general had a poor opinion of her. However, once the mediation program received adequate publicity and the student's status as a mediator was revealed, her relationship with all teachers improved. She also reported that her own behavior improved.

Some students took strong exception to the suggestion that teachers would have a necessarily higher or even changed opinion of students due to their status as mediators. For example, "I have to disagree . . . that mediation makes teachers look at you differently. I think it's what you put out and what they take in. I have been doing [positive] stuff since my sophomore year and no teacher has ever changed their opinion because of that. I think it's when you give out respect and the way you present yourself to them. . . . They may take it in as 'Oh look, she's trying hard,' or 'I just do not like her.'"

A number of students in one particular focus group used the group to complain about teacher-student relations in general. Several anecdotes described individual teacher decisions that were not subject to mediation and the frustration the mediators felt at their subsequent disempowerment. For instance: "I had a problem with my English teacher because I couldn't take a test. I said, 'Can I make up the test' and she said, 'No, you can't.' She just said, 'Go sit down.'. . . You can't talk to her because she is a teacher and you are a student." In this particular situation, when the student says "you can't talk to her" she seems to mean "I can't talk to her the way I would like to." In fact, several students from different high schools commented on the difficulty of mediating with teachers as one of the parties. One mediator summed up her changed relationship with teachers as a result of participating in peer mediation by stating that "teacher[s] give me the same respect that I give them. I treat them the way I want to be treated."

Emotional states

The final broad theme of change concerns the mediators' internal emotional states. Several mediators, when asked to identify important changes that have occurred since mediating, stated that they felt calmer, happier, mellower, and more outgoing. One mediator stated quite frankly that "mediation makes me feel good because sometimes you look out [at the parties in mediation] . . . and there are some guys that are so popular . . . you sort of stand to one side because you're not as popular. And then you are called down to mediate and who do you find in the mediation? You find those guys and they're fighting about simple things and that makes you feel good because you help them and they look at you differently. . . ." Being a mediator and participating in peer mediation seems to have improved the self-esteem of students who may not have previously found a positive school role.

Conclusion

Through the survey and focus groups, this study suggests that many of the skills and attitudes commonly associated with mediating qualities may be the same as we expect to see in effective leaders. Mediators identified a number of important skill areas and changes in their lives that resulted from peer mediation training and participation in the mediation program that can be compared to the elements of leadership identified by Woyach (1992) and to the relationship identified by Rost (1991) as essential to leadership development.

Woyach stated that the elements of leadership development are "essential for individuals to organize themselves, establish goals and priorities, make decisions, settle conflicts, and accomplish their goals" (1992, p. 3). This is precisely what mediators do. Mediators are responsible for the organization of the mediation process that provides critical information about a conflict and is designed to accomplish the goals of the parties to reach resolution. Organizing the process is important in order for mediators to work effectively with students to help settle conflicts.

The participants in this study identified some of the elements that enable mediators to successfully mediate conflicts among their peers. In the process, they identified elements of personal growth and development that enabled them to function as leaders. The elements identified by the mediators that emerged during the focus group discussions were neutrality, self-control, personal efficacy, understanding the perceptions of others, and improved emotional states. As mediators make decisions and set priorities regarding the mediation process, and as they develop trusting relationships with the parties by maintaining a neutral or objective status, clearly they exhibit leadership.

The five themes that emerged from the focus groups pointed to changes in feelings and attitudes that mediators identified as resulting from skills developed during training or observations made during mediation. During a mediation, mediators have an opportunity to observe the effects of increased positive communication between the parties, and how listening to the other side of the story and discussing the issues can begin to change how the parties view the situation in which they find themselves. The benefits of positive communication for the mediators transfers to other situations as mediators experiment with new communication techniques with friends and family members.

One of the most impressive areas of growth or change identified by the mediators was in the area of personal efficacy. Personal efficacy included being responsible as a mediator to facilitate the process of mediation for the parties, being responsible for role-modeling positive conflict resolution for the school, getting involved in leadership roles in the school, developing an awareness of and interest in career or future goals, and improving communication skills and interpersonal relationships. During the focus group sessions, mediators felt that acting in a responsible manner and improving their communication skills were elements of personal efficacy that provided mediators with the greatest sense of self-esteem, pride in themselves as mediators, and pride in their relationships with others.

Efficacy also emerged as a theme from the survey. As mediators become more comfortable with their mediation skills, they identified the "best thing about being a mediator" as the change in how they viewed themselves and the change in their relationships with other people. Mediators viewed themselves as being more patient, capable people who can be trusted and respected by both their peers and adults for "doing the right thing," as well as for "doing things right." According to Rost (1991), leadership is the process that develops the connections among leaders and followers, and the followers expect that their leaders will know what the right thing

is and then do it. He feels that the process of developing this connection—how leaders and followers relate to one another—is key
to leadership.

Like Rost, the mediators in this study described many of their
mediation activities in relational terms. They agreed on the survey
that they related differently to their peers, valued changes in their
relationships with their peer, and demonstrated more patience
when listening to both sides of the story. As mediators developed
stronger interpersonal skills, formed trusting relationships with
peers and adults, and advocated nonviolent resolution to conflict
as a result of being trained as mediators and participating in the
peer mediation program, they became more effective in their role
as mediators both in school and at home. The skills and sensitivities that enable mediators to mediate successfully or "help" settle
conflicts enabled them to function also as leaders.

Due to a gap in the literature in how student leadership is developed, this study, as well as future studies in the area of leadership
development for students, can begin to help program coordinators,
teachers, and school administrators identify some of the leadership
skills that are developing in students as a result of participation in
specific school programs and learning opportunities. Once educators are aware of the leadership potential these programs and learning opportunities provide for students, they can guide students
toward activities that will enhance both their personal and their
academic lives. When students provide the definition of leadership,
identify the skills of student leaders, and describe how the definition applies to their specific situations, educators can begin to use
that definition of leadership, incorporate leadership skills development into the curriculum and other activities in school, and teach
students to be leaders.

References

Allen, R. F. *A Dispute Mediation Program: Report on Cobble Middle School.* Tal-
    lahassee: State of Florida, 1993. (ED 368 643)
Bush, R.A.B. "Transformative Mediation in Theory and Practice: Why It
    Matters and What It Takes." Paper presented at meeting of the Massachu-

setts Association of Mediation Programs and Practitioners, Brandeis University, Waltham, Mass., Apr. 1995.

Bush, R.A.B., and Folger, J. P. *The Promise of Mediation: Responding to Conflict through Empowerment and Recognition.* San Francisco: Jossey-Bass, 1994.

Cutrona, C., and Guerin, C. "Confronting Conflict Peacefully." *Educational Horizons*, 1994, 72(2), 95–104.

Johnson, D. W., and Johnson, R. T. *Reducing School Violence Through Conflict Resolution.* Alexandria, Va.: Association for Supervision and Curriculum Development, 1995.

Krueger, R. A. *Focus Groups: A Practical Guide for Applied Research.* Thousand Oaks, Calif.: Sage Publications, 1988.

Patton, M. Q. *How to Use Qualitative Methods in Evaluation.* Thousand Oaks, Calif.: Sage Publications, 1987.

Prothrow-Stith, D. *Deadly Consequences: How Violence Is Destroying Our Teenage Population and a Plan to Begin Solving the Problem.* New York: HarperCollins, 1991.

Rost, J. C. *Leadership for the Twenty-First Century.* Westport, Conn.: Praeger, 1991.

Woyach, R. B. *Leadership in Civic Education.* Washington, D.C.: Office of Educational Research and Improvement, 1992. (ED 351 270)

PATRICIA ENSELL TRELA is a doctoral student and research assistant at the University of Massachusetts Lowell and a mediator for community and family mediation programs in Massachusetts and New Hampshire.

MICHAEL J. CONLEY is a doctoral student at the University of Massachusetts Lowell and a special education teacher at Mascenic Regional High School in Ipswich, New Hampshire.

This chapter explores nontraditional student leadership through the eyes of two students who made their impact outside the traditional roles offered in most high schools. The brief introduction and conclusion by Tracey Schaub tie together the two stories by Sukanya Lahiri and John Laurence Auerbach by examining the implications and benefits of two different nontraditional student leadership experiences.

8

The development of nontraditional student leadership

Tracey Schaub, Sukanya Lahiri,
John Laurence Auerbach

STUDENT LEADERSHIP COMES IN ALL PACKAGES, not just the typical student council president or captain of the football team. True leadership is generated from within students and by their actions, not by their titles. On the surface, Sukanya Lahiri and John Auerbach could not be more different. Sukanya lives in an upper-middle-class town outside of Boston, where she graduated from the local high school. Her interests reside in multicultural issues and peace education. John graduated from a private high school in the South and is a business entrepreneur. These two young people come from different backgrounds, yet they both excelled in the area of student leadership. Neither Sukanya or John had a clear vision early on about leadership, or a specific sense of direction regarding their potential contributions to society and their schools. Their desire to get involved stemmed from early interests that they parlayed

NEW DIRECTIONS FOR SCHOOL LEADERSHIP, NO. 4, SUMMER 1997 © JOSSEY-BASS PUBLISHERS

into, respectively, global involvement in multicultural issues and a successful business venture. Sukanya and John did not become leaders overnight. They were encouraged by teachers and family members to pursue opportunities and take risks to meet new challenges.

Not all students will develop as leaders within the structure of a school system. In the past, this has meant excluding a lot of students from exploring their potential for leadership. All opportunities for leadership and contribution must be encouraged and embraced if schools are going to utilize students as resources for leadership. Sukanya and John are excellent examples of true student leadership. Neither one had a title or a specific job to do. Both were able to benefit from a string of small successes and create a foundation from which to draw upon when faced with more difficult challenges. Sukanya's and John's leadership experiences, confidence, and perseverance have led them to where they are today: Sukanya is a student at Harvard University and is continuing to develop her interests in peace education, and John is a student at Duke University while continuing to run his computer company.

The following stories were written by Sukanya and John to illustrate their perspectives on their unique student leadership experiences. These two people represent a minority of students who are able to develop leadership skills outside the school system. It is important to note that although these two students were involved in outside projects, the support and guidance they received from within their schools was of great encouragement to them. Sukanya's and John's stories provide insight into the potential for development of student abilities through nontraditional means.

Sukanya's story

During my freshman year in high school I became an active member of my school's Multicultural Issues Group. It was founded to direct positive change toward increased understanding of the differences among people and the acceptance of those differences by the student body. The group's mission was "to provide an environment in which people are valued, accepted, and appreciated; to provide forums for open dialogue; and to foster understanding and acceptance of differences" (Winchester Community Multicultural Network, 1994). It was through the intensive training, the workshops, and the open dialogue that I became aware of the ability of one person to make a difference.

A greater understanding of the power of effective leadership came when I was a facilitator and staff trainer of a program called Into the Circle: Teens Teaching the Green Circle program. This program facilitates an understanding of human differences and similarities and promotes a positive sense of self-worth and a greater sense of empathy in second-grade children. I believe that the best way to work toward creating a more peaceful society is to instill positive values in children. This program, sponsored by a nonprofit human relations organization, the National Conference, works to instill these values in a fun and effective manner. After attending a two-day intensive training workshop, I began teaching the program as a freshman in high school.

As I saw these children's horizons widen and their circles of acceptance grow, I recognized my own growth as well. I learned the importance of initiative as I helped to get the Green Circle program incorporated into the Winchester Public School System. The challenge was also a lesson in perseverance, trying and retrying to convince teachers, principals, and the school committee of the benefits of the program despite the consequent loss of class time for the high school students who serve as facilitators and for the elementary school students. Through diligence and hard work on our part, the program was accepted by the school population. I am especially proud of the growth of the Green Circle program in my community: in 1993, my partner and I were Winchester's only facilitators; in January of 1995, with the able guidance of a revered community leader, we had townwide training and a total of nine facilitators.

In my sophomore year of high school I was very fortunate to be able to participate in the Green Circle National Conference's

week-long multicultural leadership camp called ANYTOWN. ANY-
TOWN facilitates a search and investigation of one's own prejudices,
biases, and beliefs. I learned that for me to be able to help and teach
others, I must first be introspective and learn about myself. One
source for introspection and strength was the National Conference
Youth Council, which consisted of Green Circle facilitators and
ANYTOWN graduates.

It was through the National Conference Youth Council newsletter that I received an application for the Elie Wiesel Foundation
for Humanity's Conference entitled, Tomorrow's Leaders: A Young
People's Conference on International Understanding. I was
selected as one of six representatives for the United States. The
conference was held in Venice, Italy, and six students were present
from five regions of critical conflict in the world: Bosnia-Herze-
govina, Ireland, Africa, the Middle East, and the United States.
While the many distinguished world leaders who were present
offered words of wisdom, the most valuable lessons were learned
from my peers.

At the International Understanding conference, my peers and I
grappled with our struggles, both internal and inherited, and we
intimately shared our sufferings, fears, and dreams. This sharing
renewed our sense of hope and faith in our ability to search for
more humane responses to conflicts, even after centuries of war.
While the issues we face may seem overwhelming and daunting at
times, we learned that every effort can make a significant difference. To make a difference, we must build on precedence and recognize the reality of the drip-drop effect. While one person's efforts
may be but a drop, with others following, supporting, and initiating, the drop becomes a drip, the drip becomes a stream, the stream
becomes a river, and finally the river becomes the ocean.

Each of us can be that drop; we can each make a difference.
With honest communication, teamwork, understanding, perseverance, and initiative coupled with resources and organized support,
a leader can direct others toward positive change. A true leader
inspires and encourages others to embrace all challenges eagerly as
opportunities for personal growth and positive change.

John's story

You don't have to be the class president to play an important role in school affairs and in the community. Since the time my grandfather gave me my first computer at age two I have developed my personal interest in technology, especially computers, culminating in the start of a successful business. I decided to start Vision Computer Services in 1992 when I was attending a summer program in computers at a local school. My teachers, Cheryl Rodgers and Jim Diez, were trying to choose equipment for the next school year at that time. I made some suggestions and helped them, and then asked myself, Why not take this one step further and actually sell them the equipment? In 1992, when I was thirteen years old, I received my first business license and Vision Computer Services became an official company. Realizing my interest in computers, my teachers at the Westminster Schools in Atlanta, Georgia, gave me not only encouragement but also support in my endeavors. Whether it was rearranging my schedule or accompanying me to business dinners, Westminster demonstrated its backing. In addition, my family has also been very supportive of my venture. Without their help and support it would have been very difficult, if not impossible, to start and run a successful business. This constant support from both my school and my family gave me the confidence to take the risks necessary to be successful. Persistence also played an important role in the success of my business and as a leader. There were a number of times when some business transaction would go wrong or the business itself would get very tedious, but I was always confident in my ability to solve the problem.

Today, Vision Computer sells computer hardware and software to schools in six southern states. My willingness to research products and learn about applications of hardware and software are two aspects of Vision Computer that my clients find valuable. I regularly read technology journals and attend computer conferences and trade shows, including Comdex and MacWorld Exposition. My research efforts and advice, coupled with very competitive pricing and youthful enthusiasm, make Vision Computer Services unique

among its competitors. I have gone from providing service to one
school, Pace Academy, to providing it to many schools, including
Midsouth Independent Schools Business Officers Purchasing Con-
sortium's fifty-six schools. Although I am not a person who seeks
publicity, my entrepreneurship has been recognized in numerous
publications, and most recently in a video for fifth graders.

A milestone for my business was receiving the Youth Entrepreneur Award from the Atlanta Association for Corporate Growth.
The award goes to the winner of a citywide competition that seeks
a local high school student currently operating his or her own business. Winning this prestigious award was both an honor and an
opportunity. It enabled me to meet some of Atlanta's business leaders, who shared their own avenues to success.

More than a ceremonial acknowledgment of hard work, the
award was an opportunity for me to observe how the different talents, career paths, and educational backgrounds of the business
leaders allowed them to be successful. I saw how they took advan-
tage of opportunities in their lives and their businesses, breaking
down barriers and pushing back horizons. Using these business
leaders as examples, I look forward to an opportunity to prepare
for a future with endless possibilities. As a fellow graduate once
said, "Life has an infinite number of possibilities, and the boundaries that exist are only temporary."

Conclusion

It is clear from these two stories that true leadership does not come
with a title or directions. John and Sukanya made a real difference
in their schools and communities at a very young age, and they
continue to make an impact. Nontraditional leadership will continue to be a sparse entity among students, until administrators and
teachers take the lead. This issue will continue to be on the back
burner until faculties see the benefits of developing and supporting students in nontraditional roles. Motivated and committed faculty are needed to explore, research, develop, implement, and

maintain innovative programs. The leadership experiences in high schools that Sukanya and John wrote about are few and far between. They have brought the issue to the table, but unfortunately the surface of the issue has barely been scratched.

Reference

Winchester Community Multicultural Network. *One Thousand and One Ways to Celebrate Multiculturalism.* Winchester, Mass.: Winchester Community Multicultural Network, 1994.

TRACEY SCHAUB is an adjunct faculty member and doctoral student at the University of Massachusetts Lowell.

SUKANYA LAHIRI is a graduate of Winchester High School, Winchester, Massachusetts, and is currently a student at Harvard-Radcliffe College.

JOHN LAURENCE AUERBACH is a graduate of The Westminster Schools, Atlanta, Georgia, and is currently a student at Duke University.

The activities, words, and philosophies of two high school principals as they cope with the challenges of supporting student leadership in two very different school settings are shared in this chapter. Common themes emerge from interviews and are summarized in a framework of guiding ideas, attitudes and skills, and responsive infrastructure. The framework is a tool that any educator can use to advance his or her understanding of and effectiveness in fostering student leadership.

9

The view from the principal's desk

Chuck Christensen

AS A UNIVERSITY TEACHER AND SCHOOL CONSULTANT, I work closely with school administrators, but the topic of student leadership seldom comes up. So I decided to interview two school principals to find out their views on student leadership in the contemporary landscape of schools and educational reform. Along the way, I also had the opportunity to observe the following student leadership activities in each principal's school.

Scene: The Bromfield School. Twenty students had filtered into the cafeteria and most were sipping orange juice or coffee from white styrofoam cups. Some were still at the refreshment table putting cream cheese on bagels. Mihran Keoseian, the principal, was chatting with several of the community people in attendance as he set up a flip chart containing an agenda for the meeting. A faculty member sat at a table with a team of students comparing and discussing notes from their previous meeting. It was 7:15 A.M.

NEW DIRECTIONS FOR SCHOOL LEADERSHIP, NO. 4, SUMMER 1997 © JOSSEY-BASS PUBLISHERS

I was observing one in a series of student working meetings devoted to the school's vision statement. This morning, three of eight task groups composed of several students and an adult would offer their progress reports. During the report of the communication skills group a student commented, "If we were really serious about communication at the school, our group felt, it should be two-way. Students should evaluate with teachers how their courses are going." A parent from another group chimed in: "I support the idea of students evaluating teachers." Then another student from the communications group offered, "Well it's not really evaluation. It's more like feedback. But it should be two-way."

By the time student traffic picked up through the cafeteria as homeroom was about to begin, three groups had reported. Principal Keoseian encouraged discussion from all the students present as well as from the adults. Attitudes, questions, assumptions, and feelings were vigorously exchanged. A date for the next meeting was established. As students shuffled their belongings into knapsacks, I observed two students and a parent exchanging e-mail addresses so they could communicate more effectively.

Scene: Lowell High School. It was a cold February morning. Eight students, the student activities coordinator, and a volunteer university consultant left the headmaster's office to walk the five busy blocks down Main Street to the third floor offices of the Lowell Plan, a local business initiative supporting community improvement. Bill Samaras, the headmaster of the high school, had arranged for the Lowell Plan to provide their conference room facilities to the group. He had combined student government leaders with senior class officers, and he had assigned another student appointee from his Headmaster's Advisory Council to spend the day considering their roles as leaders at Lowell High School. How could they improve their collaboration and deal with a difficult transition period caused by a major renovation and construction program at the high school?

By the time pizza and cokes arrived for a lunch break, the group had created a mission statement, designed some improvements to their meeting and communication procedures, and ironed out some interpersonal differences. They had begun to formulate recommendations for the headmaster regarding restructuring of student leadership at the school, better use of the energy and enthusiasm generated by the large number of school clubs, and improved coordination. The university consultant offered observations and suggestions along the way. The meeting reflected Samaras's vital concern that student leadership continue to be an important dimension of life at the high school as burgeoning enrollments, an increasingly diverse student body, and the building construction project exerted pressure on everyone.

These two scenes took place at two very demographically different schools. Let me introduce the two school principals before sharing their interview responses.

Mihran Keoseian is principal of the Bromfield School in Harvard, Massachusetts. Bromfield is a grades 7 through 12 public school of five hundred students in a rural-suburban, upper-middle-class town of 5,000 residents. Mihran has been in education for twenty-six years and has been a school leader in four different school districts.

Bill Samaras is headmaster of Lowell High School in Lowell, Massachusetts. With its three thousand students in grades 9 through 12, Lowell High is the single public high school in this multiethnic, working-class city of approximately 98,000 residents. Bill's educational career spans thirty-three years. He attended Lowell High School as a student.

My conversations with these school leaders were held separately at their respective schools. Because there was a striking similarity of concerns and themes, I have melded their comments together here for the ease of the reader. The views from the two principals' desks are revealed in their comments.

Conversations with two principals

CC: *How would you define student leadership?*

SAMARAS: There are several definitions of student leadership. But I'd identify a student leader as any student that would have an impact on the school. That student would motivate other students to take a position, to react to some situation and feel they could actually make a difference.

KEOSEIAN: Students shouldn't be allowed to call themselves leaders unless they have made an impact in what goes on in school, a noticeable difference in the culture of the school, on the actual learning taking place in the school, or the governance of the school. The key word is *impact*.

SAMARAS: A lot of students feel that they can't make a difference because there's nobody out there to listen to them. They feel they have very little impact on school life.

KEOSEIAN: What I try to do is push students to recognize that if they truly want to be a student leader they need to be actively engaged in helping make that impact, not just getting the prom under way. While that is important, I wouldn't put it in the same category of student leadership.

CC: *It sounds like student leadership is not necessarily related to an office, position, or title. It's more of an* activity *having to do with the student's impact or influence on those around him and on the life of the school. What is the most important aspect of student leadership?*

KEOSEIAN: I think it goes back to the administrators and teachers. There has to be a true belief that kids do make a difference. If that is evident, then the kids take it seriously. I've seen a lot of kids enter the administrative office with either a written petition or an important thought and they're usually paid lip service and they just go away and see that nothing happens. So it really has to come from the adults first, that is, the belief that students really can make a difference.

SAMARAS: Yes, for it to work, the students have to know that the administration is not going to give them lip service. If they feel that we're giving lip service, they'll walk away from us. Then there are two things they can do. One, they can just walk away from us and forget it. They can become nondescript; they do their thing for the short period of time, get their name in the paper and the graduation list, but contribute nothing. Or they can become adversaries if they don't feel they are being listened to. Some students will fight you to the wire because they don't believe in you and they feel you don't believe in them. It's critical that you make sure the students know that you are listening even if you disagree with them.

CC: *You made a good point about the importance of students feeling it's not just lip service, but that they will be listened to and how much goes into that. What other hurdles exist?*

SAMARAS: Apathy. Sometimes we don't have students with the time to dedicate themselves toward student leadership or getting involved. Many work. Others are involved in multiple sports or activities. Apathy is also tied in with, "I don't think I can make a difference." We take for granted sometimes that high school students know what to do. We always have to remember that they are high school students and they need to be trained and supported. So some of the apathy may come from never being trained.

KEOSEIAN: I think we make a gross error in this business when kids get elected to student council or whatever and we say now you're a leader. They believe that and they fatten up resumes for applying to colleges or seeking scholarships. But when asked what they've done to demonstrate their leadership, they are uncertain. Of course, we adults are still struggling in schools to understand what leadership is as well.

SAMARAS: I have had many student government and class presidents that have had a great impact on the school. They had natural leadership skills and with a little help from us they became even better. Then there were those who had the desire and the heart but not the skill. I sent them to workshops and built up their confidence by getting them involved with more situations, especially with adults. But still, for some it didn't click. Maybe they were nervous. They were nice enough students, they didn't disgrace us, but really added very little to the school. That's when I went to people who had a lot of personal power who didn't get elected but had the desire to make a change.

CC: *So sometimes there's a fortunate overlap between the popularity of students getting into office and their actual leadership skills. Other times it may not happen and you have to cultivate additional student leaders and make spaces for them to participate.*

SAMARAS: A student recently shared with me that although he did not get elected to office, he felt he had the personal power and drive of a leader. He works with a large group of students who follow him. He's trying to make a difference. Right now he's confused as to understanding what personal power means, if you don't have elective power. I'm working with him to develop his leadership skills, which he certainly does have.

CC: *How do you help to include students when they don't have the positional power of an elected office?*

SAMARAS: One way is by setting up committees for certain projects or pulling together groups of kids. We had a difficult situation where students were paying more money to park their cars in a public facility than teachers were. We got a group of local businesspeople to come to the high school, and an ad hoc group of students were willing to speak out about the issue. They followed up with a meeting with the mayor and the school board. The kids handled themselves very well and succeeded in changing the situation.

In another instance a young lady in a wheelchair, who not only was very well liked but also had a strong sense of life and purpose, came right through the office and went directly to me and said, "You better listen because I don't think you're aware of what's going on!" She had a deep concern about the fact that some students couldn't get to me to be heard. I had some knowledge about what she was talking about, and I gave her my opinions. I found her to be someone who could listen and understand. After that we started a great relationship, and she became an advocate for a whole group of students who didn't have a forum.

KEOSEIAN: You need to actively create opportunities for students to get involved. When I first came to this school there were numerous student groups that wanted to do something, but no one was coordinating this or helping specify roles. I held four evening meetings to bring students together to sift and sort through what was happening. Interestingly, the kids insisted that these workshops continue and we ended up having eight evening workshops which helped bring clarity as to who wanted to do what, and more importantly, how they could get it done. These sessions were not limited to elected student leaders. They provided opportunity to many students.

Another example of an opportunity was this. Last year in light of budget decreases and the institution of user fees for sports and activities we held a series of workshops for kids and oriented them to the budget development process. Local and state presenters helped us. I laid some groundwork to guide student thinking to consider not just what they liked or wanted but what was good for the school as a whole. Subsequently, the kids did a superior job of grilling town leaders and school board representatives. Then they helped me put together a truly grassroots budget. Those that came forward were listened to, and they understood circumstances a lot better than when we first started.

CC: *What are some other conditions that need to be present for a true expression of student leadership?*

SAMARAS: Openness. Disagreements are inevitable. I found myself in one case discussing an issue with the students where kids were coming in late or leaving the school to eat at this local restaurant. I threatened to put pressure on the restaurant and possible legal action. Yet the owners were very nice, decent people. In one confrontation, the students got very upset with me and I got upset with them. I recall going home and still being upset. I sat down and replayed the whole conversation and tried to analyze how they were looking at things. I tried to understand what mistakes I made and what mistakes I didn't make. I asked to meet with them again and I apologized for not listening as much as I should have. They in turn apologized for going a little beyond the respect area for my position. I did have legitimate concerns. To let them know that I wasn't just being arbitrary and capricious, we did have someone intervene—a teacher who had a good relationship with me and the students. She was seen as a very fair negotiator between us.

I learned a lot from that. I learned if you have strong opinions about an issue you might be meeting with a group that have equally strong opinions. How do you communicate and negotiate? Coming to consensus requires very mature thinking, which I was fortunate to have with some of the students.

KEOSEIAN: Another condition for student leadership is training. Students need training, some type of planned approach: providing information, developing skills, and creating opportunities for kids to feel their way through what type of leaders they want to be. I often comment that leadership comes in many packages. Typically, we as human beings suffer from the stereotype of a leader—a charismatic figure, maybe on a white horse with the wind blowing their hair back, someone who stands out from the crowd. I try to get kids to realize that to be true leaders they are a servant and debtor. You're really serving other people. And if you're blessed to have leadership qualities, you should be involved in paying back. The true leader needs to be humble and thankful for the good leadership qualities they have. I use this notion in the workshops I do with the kids. You know, no white horses here.

CC: *And the exploration of those ideas happens in the deliberate approach to training you've been talking about.*

KEOSEIAN: Start with true belief in the students. Then support and training are paramount.

CC: *What's the most difficult thing regarding student leadership?*

KEOSEIAN: Interestingly enough, kids have a hard time when they realize they can make decisions and changes that will have an impact—even affecting curriculum. Or when they realize they can make a decision that affects teachers, it's almost that the process slows down a bit. Many of these kids revere their teachers. Students at another school where I worked were involved in establishing an attendance policy and revising graduation requirements. As we got very close to a final decision—cold feet. They asked who is going to convey this to the student body and I said, "*We* are." They had a very hard time with that. Although they believed in the new policies, they had some real issues about taking leadership to its max. They realized it would cause conflict between them and their peers.

Currently at this school I've included three students on our scheduling study committee. They've been on every committee visitation to other schools and we have one meeting left and it's decision time. Now I'm seeing concerns surface with them (by the way, the same is true with staff). So, who will finally stand up and say this is what we believe in and why? And this is what we have decided. Kids have a hard time making decisions that affect their peers and also their teachers. It's, "Oh, we didn't really want to go that far with it." But true leadership is being there, not just in the beginning, but also in the end. Again, kids deserve support all along the way.

CC: *What other initiatives are you currently trying to develop at this school?*

KEOSEIAN: We are undertaking a major initiative that is moving an eight-point vision statement about student competencies into an action plan. Students are working with volunteer adults from the community and some faculty to define and understand each of the eight points, such as using critical thinking and problem solving, communicating clearly, and being socially responsible. They will gather examples from their own and their peers' experiences throughout the school. Then they will help us to assess the curriculum and identify where we are or are not teaching critical thinking, developing communication skills, or fostering social responsibility. My belief is the kids can do this with proper training and support. This is a lot different from preparing a prom. This is truly getting into the heart and core of teaching and learning in our school. And the kids want to be part of it.

I've always involved the kids in important school issues. Student leadership is really an untapped potential; you'd be astonished that these kids bring such good insights to the change process. They should have significant roles in school improvement.

CC: *Anything else that you'd like to comment on?*

SAMARAS: I think we have our students pretty well involved in school, but we could do much more. And I wonder about our consistency. Every year we get a new group of freshmen in and I welcome them, but I have to paint a picture as to what their potential can be. I paint a vision of what their role should be at the high school and how they should be behaving when they leave. It isn't just about getting into college. It's more than that. You have a potential to make a change at this high school that will also affect how you will handle yourselves in the world of work and further schooling. And each year I have to have something for them to do from sophomore to junior year and finally senior year. Senior year is a short year. After March, seniors are just preparing for graduation. Many lose their eagerness or zealousness. But then my students who have been trained, my best, have followed through right to the end. They become mentors to the new juniors coming in. I've pretty much ironed a model to take those freshmen right through to seniors and have a lot of kids involved. But it's a constantly renewing process.

KEOSEIAN: I've often been asked what my ultimate goal is in working so much with student leaders. I want all staff members to recognize that each student, regardless of ability level, should in part, not totally, help design the outcomes of all our courses and programs. I'm convinced that they will make even higher demands on the instructional program than we currently do. And this school has a very receptive staff compared to others I have worked with. But the students need us to believe in them, they need the confidence we can give them, and they need the training and groundwork to be provided. That's where we're heading. That's my ultimate goal. Catch me in four years and see how we're doing.

CC: *Thank you, and we'll keep in touch.*

Toward an architecture of student leadership

What is student leadership, really? More importantly, how can we release its untapped potential in improving our schools? This chapter began to explore these questions by listening to the views of two different principals in two remarkably different school districts. Yet I found the similarities of their ideas and sentiments about student leadership striking. Furthermore, after my conversations with Bill Samaras and Mihran Keoseian, I am convinced that the principal is the prime catalyst in developing student leadership.

How can principals think and act more strategically if they are serious about exploring and harnessing the potential of student leadership? Is there a framework for focusing their thinking and acting? In his writings on learning organizations, Peter Senge

(1990, 1994) suggests that leaders should think of themselves as architects. They need to design structures for programs such as student leadership deliberately if these programs are to grow and flourish. Senge suggests that, as in architecture, leaders should consider generic design elements to guide their thinking. He poses three elements: guiding ideas, attitudes and skills, and a responsive infrastructure. Remove or weaken any one of these design elements and the structure quivers or collapses. There is an integrity to the three-element architecture. We can review the themes that emerged from my conversations with the principals within this architectural metaphor and sketch out these design elements.

First, *guiding ideas* are an essential element. Without guiding ideas there is no passion. Ideas grab people. They provide a sense of purpose worthy of our commitment. They suggest direction. On the basis of my conversations with Keoseian and Samaras I have identified three seminal guiding ideas:

1. Adults need to truly believe that students are capable of significant leadership roles in schools. Lip service will not do.
2. Student leadership should have an impact on significant aspects of school life, such as climate, curriculum, instruction, and governance. Planning the prom and sponsoring activities are not enough.
3. Leadership needs to be viewed as an activity in which any student can participate. It is not limited to an office or position. It does not automatically arise from an election.

How can we help these ideas come to life in a school?

Attitudes and skills are a second design element of the architecture. In the arena of day-to-day activity, actions are driven by attitudes and derive their impact from skillful behavior. The right attitudes and skills breathe life into the guiding ideas. Thoughts are translated into effective action. Instead of managing appearances, we move to achieve what we value.

It is evident in both principals' conversations that they take quite seriously their role in cultivating student attitudes. They enlist and encourage students to truly feel that they are being listened to and that they can make a difference. When students have no awareness that they can be leaders and make a difference, their attitude is apathy. When there is apathy there is no attempt to lead.

But positive student attitudes, while necessary, are not sufficient to infuse a school with student leadership. Skills are required. Both Keoseian and Samaras coach and cajole students to develop the skills of listening and communicating clearly, of being reflective about their leadership behaviors, and of articulating the needs of all students, not just their own. They foster students' ability to see things from other people's points of view. They provide support for students to nurture attitudes and develop skills.

A *responsive infrastructure* completes the architectural integrity of the design elements. Guiding ideas, attitudes, and skillful actions must be expressed within the organizational context of a school. What does the school infrastructure allow? Are there resources and opportunities for students to develop the right attitudes and skillful behaviors? Principals Samaras and Keoseian offer deliberate, continuing opportunities for students to discover, learn, and refine their skills. They give more than lip service to the paramount importance of training for student leaders; they provide for it. Students also need information about school policies, budgets, curriculum, legal issues, and political practice if they are to act intelligently and perform with savvy. Both principals create opportunities for students to interact with local political leaders, with adults from the community, with administrators, and with faculty members to gain important information directly and to understand that there are multiple perspectives.

Student leadership requires time. Time is one of the most precious resources for students and adults. In schools, time is tightly scheduled. Yet principals must design the school infrastructure to include well-run meetings before, during, and after school hours. Defining agendas and formally scheduling faculty members or community leaders to be present at meetings or forums also helps to address the time crunch. Additionally, administrators must balance the mountain of competing demands for their own time and attention to protect the time necessary to really listen to students informally and in spontaneous circumstances. Samaras's anecdotes clearly illustrated his openness to student concerns. Keoseian extended four evening workshops to eight when he saw the response.

And what about impact? "The prom needs to get planned, but. . . ." Beyond the prom, Keoseian has consciously structured the involvement of student leaders in examining and testing his school's vision statement. Thus his infrastructure includes opportunities for students to consider and work on issues of real significance to the school. Students are deliberately involved with teachers and community members in influencing decisions about curriculum and instruction. This orchestrated involvement honors the guiding ideas about student leadership just described and counteracts apathy and cynicism. But these efforts need to be designed.

Designing responsive infrastructures to support student leadership may be the least understood of the three design elements. We need to discover and share additional promising practices in this area. For instance, we are just beginning to explore technology such as e-mail to make the school's infrastructure more responsive. This may increase access for more people across different role groups. It may lead to more thoughtful opinion sharing and timely communication.

I enjoyed my conversations with principals Keoseian and Samaras, observing at their schools, and learning about their views and aspirations in the area of student leadership development. They revealed many of the complexities and challenges that principals must face if they are to tap the potential of student leadership to support school improvement.

Principals are the chief architects in this enterprise, and without deliberate attention to the design elements outlined here, real student leadership will not happen. The existing landscapes, raw materials, and preliminary foundations will vary for different principals in different schools. But the challenge to create a robust architecture within which student leadership can be nurtured, strengthened, and continued cries out for committed architect-principals.

References

Senge, P. M. *The Fifth Discipline: The Art and Practice of the Learning Organization.* New York: Doubleday, 1990.

Senge, P., and others. *The Fifth Discipline Fieldbook: Strategies and Tools for Building a Learning Organization.* New York: Doubleday, 1994.

CHUCK CHRISTENSEN *is lecturer and consultant at the University of Massachusetts Lowell College of Education's Center for Field Services and Studies. He is a former principal and school board member.*

The author attempts to answer a series of questions about student leadership that complicate its expression and promotion in schools: What is leadership in schools? How is it related to broad educational goals and objectives? Can leadership be taught? Who should teach it and who should learn it? This chapter offers insights into the paradoxes and possibilities of encouraging and sustaining a level of leadership that involves every member of a group or community, and it seeks to promote the teaching of leadership as a responsibility shared equally by schools and students.

10

Leading lessons

Thomas O'Neil

The leader is vital to the direction that the team takes. That direction must be clear—and constantly referred to by players and coaches. Everyone on a team must want to go in that direction, to work together to get there. A leader is particularly responsible for the happiness of the team through his relationship with his teammates and [through] their relationship with one another. If the direction is certain and the relationships strong, then in a sense the entire team shares the responsibility of leadership—acting, advancing, and caring as one.

These comments about leadership were written by a secondary school junior, the captain of a winter athletic team. The student's insights about a complex subject—influencing and encouraging others in the advancement of shared goals and aspirations— emerged from a set of experiences that he and his teammates had as they examined, and worked at, what schools and teachers and other adults call leadership.

NEW DIRECTIONS FOR SCHOOL LEADERSHIP, NO. 4, SUMMER 1997 © JOSSEY-BASS PUBLISHERS

As a secondary school teacher, coach, administrator, and advisor, I have spent more than twenty years observing the ways in which students lead. In classes, in student government and organizations, on athletic fields, in the residential halls, and in the countless other contexts and moments that inform and define the experience of school, I have been taught important lessons in leadership from students. Indeed, the attitudes and actions of those who lead—from ninth-graders to college captains—reflect insights and abilities that may help provide useful models for a broader application of *leadership development*. In exploring these areas, I have worked extensively with one school athletic team for the past four years, and more recently I have taught an undergraduate course focusing on leadership issues at one local university and helped lead a series of seminars for team captains at another.

These experiences of working with students suggest that the development and emergence of leadership evolve from a number of factors, including context, conduct, character, and purpose. Teachers and schools are capable of identifying student leaders in various areas—academics, athletics, dramatic activities, and community service, for instance—but beyond knowing one when we see one, there are more complex issues and questions. Can leadership be developed and encouraged—and if so, who is responsible in a school setting for doing so? Are there identifiable leadership skills that can be defined and practiced? What role do power, authority, and influence play in leadership? In emphasizing leadership, are followers relegated to a secondary position and status? And in schools and for students, what is the impact of leadership on learning and development, conduct and character?

In exploring these questions, we can learn from the perspectives and experiences of our students. How do they approach and exercise leadership? And in doing so, how can they both gain insights about themselves and contribute to the experience that others gain from those classes or projects or teams or moments in their learning that help shape and define development, character, and values?

Can leadership be taught and learned?

An often-debated issue in educational and business circles, the question Can leadership be taught and learned? parallels those questions asked about ethics, morality, values, and character in schools and in society. The larger question, however, may be Where and how does a consideration of leadership fit into a student's education? When and how can students be encouraged to consider the fundamental ingredients of leadership—helping, encouraging, working together, listening, and contributing? Capable teachers and effective schools pose these questions, talk about these ideas, and therefore teach aspects of leadership in each class, in the cafeteria, at play rehearsal, and in the gym. By "teach" we mean to pose questions, to pause, and to encourage students to think about how these values affect their class or activity or project, and how their attitudes and actions advance or threaten or compromise the performance or confidence or experience of others. Students—and adults—will surely learn about leadership in many school settings; as they always do, students will listen and watch and make inferences about the world in which they are growing up. They will learn. But the question is, What conclusion will they draw about the role and relevance of empathy, of understanding, of listening, of respecting differences and different needs? And how can teachers and schools and parents help students to reflect on these matters—to reflect, weigh, and perhaps at times struggle with—and how can they ask the questions rather than provide the answers? Yes, much can be learned about leadership. And arguably the most effective way to learn is to pay attention to leadership's central components and to the value given to it throughout a school's curriculum.

In my work as coach of a winter sports team, for instance, I learned that the players, who ranged in age from fourteen to eighteen, were eager to address and discuss not only their goals and objectives for the season but also the individual and collective responsibilities that membership on the team brought. The discussions—the curriculum, as it were—involved not abstract talks about leadership but, rather, periodic conversations beginning before the season started about the purpose and point of playing. After one particularly significant session, during which strong consensus emerged about three team goals shared by all of the players, one member (interestingly, not the elected leader) suggested that each person write down these goals to refer to throughout the winter. That suggestion—that act of leadership—initiated a practice that the team has followed regularly ever since: each player keeps a journal in which he analyzes his and his team's performance, sets goals for practices and games, and considers issues relating to the development of the team and its cohesiveness. These writings contain powerful comments about aspirations, shared goals, affiliation, and collaboration—about leadership as perceived by all of the members of one team. As a teacher of English, I was struck by the relationship that developed between the players and their writing. What I had initially feared would be seen as a chore or assignment became instead an important part of daily practice. Frequently the students take their journals home to write a longer entry or to review their progress, and a number have continued the practice throughout their years on college teams. I am grateful for the suggestion made by the young player and for the leadership that it represented in integrating two seemingly separate areas of the school curriculum.

Direction

The junior captain quoted earlier alluded to the significance of *direction*. The connection between leadership and direction is critical: after all, how can there be leading without a sense of direction—a sense of where one is headed? A central component of leadership, then, is establishing a sense of purpose. What do the members of a school group or team seek through their participation? What do they aspire to achieve and experience? What do they hope to learn and how does that fit into the school's goals and aspi-rations for them?

Purpose and motive and aspiration are important issues to raise; part of leadership involves encouraging members of a group or team to consider and address these questions as a prelude to col-lective work, advancement, and direction. Again, raising these ques-tions is an act of leadership, and listening to the response of others is an equally important act and contribution. Knowing and under-standing the motives of others, helping them to articulate common and collective goals and purposes, and giving them the responsi-bility for establishing these directions are some of the highest acts of leadership. At the suggestion of the captain, for instance, the members of a high school athletic team devoted the first day of practice to a discussion of, in the words of one young player, "where we wanted to be by the end of the season and how we were all going to help each other get there." The presence of leadership on that team is evident both in the initiation of the discussion and in the consideration of "where we wanted to be"—a ninth grader's expression of purpose, motive, direction, and aspiration as he learned leadership.

Process and principle

After a direction is set, those involved in a project or endeavor must consider the question of how to get there—what route to take and what principles to follow as work is done. Will the captain or pres-ident or head—the "formal" leader—do it all, or do none of it? Will he or she command or persuade, delegate or do, decide or cajole? Will position, power, and authority inform leadership? Or will collaboration, shared motivation, and strong relationships? One of the central tasks of a leader is to understand relationships, and to recognize that the strength of relationships among members of a group—based on common interests, aspirations, and an affili-ation with others with whom they are engaged in something of value—are vital to the work that is done and the level of achievement that is realized. In a school team setting, for instance, the way in which new young members are welcomed by older players is vitally important both to the way they will perform and the inferences they will draw about the team's culture and values. Taking an interest in new members, remembering one's own experiences about the first day at a new school or the first practice on a new team, and extending oneself to others in simple ways are important and often quiet acts of leadership, informed by an appreciation of the power not of authority but of relationships.

The newest and youngest member of our team recently wrote: "The first day of practice, Geoff asked if he could warm up with me. All of his senior friends were there, but he asked me, and that made me begin to feel that I was a real part of the team." When asked later about this gesture, Geoff said simply: "I remember my first day at practice as a freshman and how much it meant when the seniors included me right away. I just wanted to continue doing that on our team."

The essence of leadership: Empathy and effort

The skills and strengths of those who lead may vary considerably depending on the contexts, terrain, and challenges of the task. But in any endeavor, two characteristics or capacities may be particularly vital to the effective exercise of leadership.

The first capacity is empathy: the ability to understand the feelings and perspectives of others, to see the world and one's relationship to it from another person's point of view. Empathy involves the ability to extend one's interest, attention, and energy to others, to recognize their motives, their worries and aspirations, their differences and commonalities, both as individuals and as members of a group, team, or class. To empathize is to listen, to connect, to be sensitive, to encourage—as suggested by Raymond Carver's short story "Put Yourself in My Shoes." Empathy is one of life's most essential emotional skills, and as such it can be developed, encouraged, and strengthened. Those in leadership positions generally possess the ability to empathize. But the larger implication for schools and students may be that emphasizing and encouraging empathy will help to create the culture and conditions that promote leadership, that foster a broad sense of understanding and interdependence among the members of a group—a principle and process that resides not in the power and purview of the "leader" but rather in the responsibilities and mutual obligations of all of those engaged in an endeavor. Empathy is a skill that gives students—and adults—insight into one of the most significant paradoxes of group performance and achievement: recognizing and respecting individual strengths and differences, which are complementary contributions, is central to collective and collaborative achievement. This winter, a player on our school team experienced some significant challenges, athletically and personally. As I was pondering how to help, a teammate of his approached me and said: "Because I have been through some of what John has going on, I spoke to him. I think what he needs most is a lot of encouragement and reminders about the confidence that we all have in him. He needs to hear how important he is not only to the team, but to all of us as his friends. If we let him know that, I think that will help him a lot." Leaders practice empathy, and empathy promotes leadership.

Beyond the capacity to empathize, leadership involves effort—the work, the time, the investment and engagement, the attitude and action, character and conduct that constitute motivation, belief, commitment, and affiliation. As every teacher and coach knows, effort is an essential element in teaching and learning. The efforts of a teacher can make a significant intellectual and developmental difference in her students; the efforts of a student can be important ingredients in his approach both to learning and to the host of other experiences and challenges that shape education, growth, and identity. Effort, then, is work—and it is also the consistent attempting, the extending of oneself, the expression of caring, the sense of trying on all levels, even in the face of difficulty and disappointment, because of a strong conviction about the value of the endeavor. Effort, and its various forms and manifestations, is arguably also a skill, and as such it can be encouraged and practiced and complimented. As with empathy, the attitudes and actions that constitute effort are at the center of the development of a broad culture of leadership, one that allows and encourages not only a few but rather everyone involved in an effort to contribute to, commit to, and invest in that effort. In that way, leaders and followers become indistinguishable; everyone, in the words of the high school captain, "shares the responsibility for leadership. Everyone helps lead."

The significance, and paradox, of this principle was underscored several years ago when Alex, the captain of our team, came to my office the day after a game. He began by saying that he had not been certain about whether to come to speak to me but had reminded himself of our earlier conversations about the responsibilities of leadership and about how those responsibilities sometimes involved speaking up about important issues even when that might be perceived as a challenge to another person's leadership or authority. He then respectfully but candidly expressed his concern about the way I had handled a particular situation the previous day. My reaction was initially defensive, but as I listened I heard articulated the very principles of leadership—effort, raising important issues, working at and through moments of challenge—upon which I had often urged the captain and players to act. Incidentally, Alex was absolutely correct in his analysis, but beyond that, the student taught both himself and his teacher a lasting lesson. To urge and encourage others to lead, we at schools need to mean it and thus occasionally face constructive reactions to our own attitudes and actions. For in speaking up, perhaps especially to us, our students are taking the very responsibilities of leadership that they have heard us urge them to assume. Leadership, then, involves both influencing and being influenced, both leading and being led.

Support for leadership

In many school settings, students hold "leadership positions." Some posts are elected, some are appointed; some are based on particular accomplishments or achievements, some on other merits or seniority. Such positions can be important, both for the individual and for the group or community. In student government, extracurricular groups, athletics, community service, and other organizations, student leaders can gain experience dealing with matters of organization, planning, and working with others. Often, however, students in those positions want and need opportunities to talk about the challenges and opportunities, the satisfaction and frustrations of their responsibilities. Teachers and schools have a tendency to recognize a student's move to leadership initially, and then to assess the student's effectiveness only when that tenure is concluded. In addition, students often express the desire to have more opportunities to discuss leadership issues and questions with their peers who have similar responsibilities.

At the suggestion of a student leader—in itself an important act of leadership—one secondary school held a series of discussions for students interested in these issues. Interestingly, the meetings were not restricted to those holding official positions; any student who had an interest was welcome to attend, and many did. These meetings became occasions to commiserate, share thoughts and strategies, and learn from the experiences of others. The response from the students was such that the concept was extended beyond that school; in the fall of 1996 the captains of all teams in the district's sixteen-member athletic league met for an evening leadership seminar and discussion. Many of the participants had competed against each other in games, but this was their first opportunity to meet in a different venue and exchange thoughts about their roles and responsibilities as captains. Here, among the students themselves, much teaching and learning took place.

Conclusion

In the college course I offer in the psychology of leadership, I once asked the class to think about moments that were particularly influential in their intellectual and personal development. Amy, a leader in every sense of the word in her high school and at college, responded almost instantly: "Eighth grade history class, the period before lunch, October 8th." Struck by the specificity of her response, the class asked Amy to elaborate. She went on to chronicle the events that had taken place that morning, describing Mrs. Stewart, her teacher and soccer coach, and the question that she had posed to that group of students eight years earlier. And very simply Amy explained the impact of that moment when, after listening to Amy's response, Mrs. Stewart "stopped, looked around the room, opened her own notebook, and wrote down what I had said. Starting then, I began to think of myself as a capable person, a girl who could contribute and help lead."

Amy and Mrs. Stewart, and the students and players who have demonstrated leadership on many levels, offer us all lessons on the subject. Ultimately, the teaching of leadership ought not to be a separate and discrete initiative in our schools but rather an integrated effort across the full range of a school's offerings. Leadership and its components can perhaps be more readily observed, identified, and complimented than formally taught, and on some levels students such as the players on the teams that it has been my privilege to learn with and from can be the most effective teachers for one another. Schools can encourage leadership by providing the time and the opportunities to discuss and promote the personal and community principles that inform effective leadership—effort, empathy, understanding, collaboration, respect, and the raising of important ethical questions that relate to matters of purpose, responsibility, conduct, and character. We can remind ourselves not to limit discussions about leadership to those who already lead, but rather to engage all of the members of institutions and communities in a consideration of the responsibilities that all share and the contributions that each can make. As teachers, we can remember both Amy's eighth-grade history class and those moments when our students exercise leadership as well as convictions—even, or indeed perhaps especially, when it comes as an occasionally warranted challenge to our own authority. For in doing so we can remind ourselves that every act of teaching involves leadership, and every act of leadership involves teaching. In these ways, then, we can help foster and encourage not only student leaders but leadership in all students.

THOMAS O'NEIL is a faculty member at Middlesex School. He is currently a visiting fellow at Harvard University and a visiting lecturer at Tufts University.

Index